P9-ASG-018

AN INTRODUCTION TO
CLASSICAL CHINESE

內政部登記證：內版台業字第一四三五號

出版者：大西洋圖書公司
　　　　台北市南昌街一段二五巷二號

發行所：大西洋圖書公司
　　　　台北市南昌街一段二五巷二號

總經銷：蘭敦圖書藝品社
　　　　台北市中山北路二段一○七號

印刷所：台元彩色印製有限公司
地　址：台北市大理街四十二巷五號
電　話：三三六七九○・三六一九八六

中華民國五十九年　　月　　日

AN INTRODUCTION TO
CLASSICAL CHINESE

by

RAYMOND DAWSON

1968

1968

ACKNOWLEDGEMENTS

SINCE it would be inappropriate to overload an introductory textbook with bibliographical footnotes, I have not acknowledged the sources which I have drawn upon in preparing this book; but it will be obvious to experts what a great debt I owe to other workers in this field. I write as one who has had some experience of the practical problems of teaching Classical Chinese rather than as a theoretical linguist, but this may not be a disadvantage since such experts sometimes contrive to make the language seem more forbidding than it really is. I am most grateful to the following colleagues and friends who have read and commented on the material in this book: A. C. Graham, M. Loewe, A. H. C. Ward, G. Dudbridge, and C. I. McMorran. I have also learnt much from my pupils, and I should particularly like to acknowledge the help of the following, who all provided me with useful comments and criticisms: I. R. Burns, Mrs. Anne Lonsdale, P. J. Reynolds, P. A. Harris, R. W. Guisso, and T. L. Whitman. They must all be exonerated from complicity in the errors which I have obstinately retained, especially as none of them was given the opportunity of checking my final version.

RAYMOND DAWSON

CONTENTS

INTRODUCTION

AT present there is a shortage of material designed to introduce the English-speaking student to the language of those important works of ancient Chinese literature which were written during the last centuries of the Chou period (4th and 3rd centuries B.C.) and had a strong formative influence on Chinese civilization. It is hoped that this book will help to remedy the situation. Although it is designed primarily to meet the needs of beginners, it may also be of use to those who know modern Chinese and wish to learn to read Classical texts.

Since Classical Chinese has an extremely simple grammar, there is no need for the student to undergo a lengthy process of linguistic initiation before he is brought face to face with a literary text. He has no conjugations or declensions to learn, no such formidable foes as gender or subjunctive to grapple with, and he can therefore, after a brief introductory description of the language and some coaching in the use of a dictionary, go straight to the heart of this remote literature, learning the grammar as he goes along. This grammar merely consists of the understanding of a few simple facts about word-order and of the use and behaviour of words which have grammatical function: difficulties mainly arise from the fact that the behaviour of some of these words is still imperfectly understood. In the learning of a language with a complicated grammar there is an obvious order of priorities, e.g. one learns the present tense before the past and the future, the indicative before the subjunctive. In Chinese there is no such priority except the obvious one of learning the most common structural principles and grammatical words first, and these will select themselves simply and naturally in the process of reading.

My procedure in this book has therefore been to choose a number of passages from the literature of the late Chou period and furnish them with a grammatical commentary.

In order not to move too slowly at the beginning I do not comment on every new feature as soon as it occurs, but where possible hold explanations over to a later stage. For similar reasons I concentrate on grammatical notes and do not cover subject matter except in the brief introductory notes to the passages. I start with five short passages from the book of Mencius, the Confucian philosopher who lived from about 370 to 290 B.C. This work is the most suitable to our purpose since the style is comparatively lucid, the text has few corruptions, and it is written in short sections suitable for excerpting. At the end of these five sections, which contain just over thirteen hundred characters, we find that we have already met a very large proportion of the constructions and grammatical words which will be encountered in this language, and we are consequently able to make a survey of the grammatical information so far obtained before proceeding to extracts from two further philosophical works, the *Mo-tzu* and *Chuang-tzu*, and two historical works, the *Kuo-yü* and *Tso-chuan*, all of which are roughly contemporary with the *Mencius*.

The language used in these five works is not, of course, precisely the same, and purists might object that it would be better to obtain a clear understanding of the grammar of one writer before proceeding to others. But I felt that it was important in a primer to illustrate the commonest features of the language of the period, no matter what authors were used; and so such questions as differences of style and dialect are largely left for the time when the beginner reaches a more sophisticated stage in his appreciation of the language.

In selecting these passages, apart from trying to ensure that all the commonest features of the language are seen in operation, I have also had regard to the question of vocabulary, which is undoubtedly the most difficult problem facing the beginner. I have tried to choose passages with a fairly limited, useful, and repetitive vocabulary, so that the student will not have to spend too much of his time in the sheer memory-work of learning characters. The text in all contains about 3,600 characters, but the total vocabulary is only about 700. I have provided a vocabulary at the back of the book so that the reader will not have to wrestle with a dictionary at the outset. Dictionaries can be very misleading, especially as they generally include definitions appropriate to all periods and types of Chinese literature, whereas my definitions pertain only to Chinese of the Classical period. My vocabulary should also be easier to use than a dictionary because it contains far fewer entries.

On looking at a Chinese book the reader is confronted with a page of characters arranged in vertical rows which he must read from top to bottom, starting with the right-hand row and working from right to left. His first problem will be to discover how to look these characters up in a dictionary or word-list.

If characters merely consisted of random conglomerations of strokes, each completely different from every other character, it would indeed be difficult to devise a principle whereby they might be arranged in sequence. But fortunately, as close inspection of the first page of text will show, there are certain elements which occur as common features of characters. Thus, for example, *tzu* 子 (1b) occurs as the top half of *Meng* 孟 (1a); 3b, 7e, and 8k all have the same element at the top; 1t and 7s both have the same right-hand element; 2c and 2i both have the same left-hand element; and the element *k'ou* 口 'mouth' appears in 1k, 1u, 1v, 2c, etc. Chinese lexicographers have picked out 214 such elements and used them as a basis for classifying all the characters in the Chinese language. These 214 elements are generally known as radicals. Thus *tzu* 子 (1b) is a radical (for all radicals can appear as characters in their own right as well as elements in other characters), and *Meng* 孟 (1a) will also be found classified under the same radical. Radicals are arranged in order according to the number of strokes with which they are written. Some guidance in the writing of characters is necessary before these strokes can be counted correctly. The student first needs to be aware of the range of strokes employed in writing Chinese characters.

These are illustrated below:

$$
\begin{array}{lll}
— & \diagdown & \diagup \\
| & \diagup & ∟ \\
\diagdown &] & ⌐ \\
\diagup & ⌊ & ⅂ \\
⌿ & ∟ & ⅃
\end{array}
$$

　　The most important stroke to remember is ⌐. It is used, for example, in the writing of the very common *k'ou* 口 element, which is written not with four strokes as the beginner might expect, but with three strokes in the following order: ⎸ ⌐ ⎯ . Similarly *yüeh* 曰 contains four strokes, not five. A glance down the first column of the text will reveal how commonly this stroke occurs: it comes in 1a, 1c, 1d, 1e, 1h, 1i, 1k, 1m, 1n, 1r, 1u, 1v, 1x, exactly half the characters. The student becomes familiar with such principles through practice at writing and looking up characters. Characters are classified under the radical according to the number of strokes additional to the radical which they contain. Thus *tzu* 子, being radical 39 without any additional strokes, will come at the beginning of the radical 39 section, but *Meng* 孟 will be classified with those characters having five additional strokes, since it is written ⌐] ⎯ 丶 ⌐ ⌿ ⎯ . The beginner will often find that he miscounts the number of strokes, but eventually traces the character he is looking for by checking through the list of characters with one more or one fewer strokes than he has calculated. It should be remembered that it is important not only to know how to count the number of strokes, but also to write the characters in the correct stroke-order. This is not as difficult as it may sound, for, as one might expect, the correct way of writing a character is generally that which lends itself to greatest fluency. Professor W. Simon's book *How to study and write Chinese Characters* will give the student valuable guidance in this matter.

　　Many characters split up like *Meng* 孟 between a top and a bottom element, and many others have a left-hand and a right-hand element, one of which is the radical. But in some the radical partially or wholly encloses the rest of the character, and in others it may be quite difficult to detect which is the radical. Accordingly for the first passage from Mencius I have indicated the radicals of all characters encountered so that the reader can begin to get the idea. The following are the main pitfalls:

　　i. Sometimes a character is composed of two or more elements, each of which does occur as a radical (e.g. the 皿 in *Meng* 孟 is radical 108). In these cases the character is only classified under one of these radicals and the student may not guess correctly first time.

　　ii. Some characters appear in an abbreviated form when they occur as radicals of other characters, e.g. radical 130 (肉) is nearly always abbreviated to what looks like radical 74 (月), so the student will often have to look under both radicals before finding the right one. The only safeguard here is to learn these abbreviated forms, and to observe in what form and where the various radicals commonly appear in the characters classified under them.

iii. There are certain irregularities with which the student gradually becomes familiar, e.g. *che* 者 is classified under radical 125 *lao* (老) although the bottom element of the radical does not appear. Characters whose radicals are not easily identifiable are listed at the end of the book under the number of strokes in the whole character.

With these notes borne in mind looking up characters is merely a matter of practice. Now a word about the pronunciations which I have been assigning these characters. Although this literature was written nearly two and a half millenniums ago, it is the general practice to read it in the modern standard pronunciation, which is based mainly on the dialect of Peking and is sometimes known as 'Mandarin'. Any other procedure is not very practicable since the reconstruction of archaic Chinese pronunciation is of necessity hypothetical and it would also be burdensome to have to learn ancient pronunciations in addition to the modern ones, which students of ancient Chinese will generally want to acquire in order to enable them to handle the modern language. The romanization which is used throughout this book is the Wade-Giles system. There are other systems which render the pronunciation much more satisfactorily than the Wade-Giles system, but it cannot be ignored by the student since it is the one commonly used in English and American sinological books as well as in dictionaries and reference works. (Since the letters of the alphabet do not represent the same sounds in all languages, other languages have necessarily had their own romanizations.) The student cannot learn to pronounce Chinese properly without expert guidance, but for the benefit of those who are working through this book on their own a rough guide to pronunciation is appended to this introduction.

One of the difficulties of learning to speak Chinese correctly is that the student not only has to learn the pronunciation of the characters, but also the tone in which they are spoken. The method of indicating the four tones when the Wade-Giles system is used is to write a superscript numeral at the end of the word, e.g. *lao*[3]. I have indicated tones in this way in the vocabulary at the end of the book, but I have not thought it worth while to mark tones throughout, since the only point in being able to pronounce Chinese absolutely correctly is to enable one to speak the language, and this book is in no way concerned with that purpose. Moreover those who learn to speak Chinese nowadays will certainly not do so by means of the Wade-Giles system.

The appearance of a character offers no direct guide to its pronunciation; but although the script is not in this sense phonetic, a great many Chinese characters do incorporate a phonetic element. It is commonly thought that Chinese is a pictographic language, but the number of true pictographs is in fact very few. *tzu* 子 is one, being originally a pictograph of a child, written thus: 孚. But the great majority of characters have an element in them which is no longer used for its pictographic meaning (if that can still be identified after the many changes which have taken place in the writing since earliest times). Thus in the word *kou* 苟 'if' the element 句 is pronounced *kou* and means a hook and is of pictographic origin, but there are several characters which have this 句 element in them merely to indicate that they share a common pronunciation with *kou* 句. An appropriate radical indicates the meaning of the various characters, e.g. *kou* 狗 (with the 'dog' radical) meaning 'dog'. In the case of *kou* 苟 'if' we have a further complication. It has the 'grass' radical and evidently meant some kind of plant, but eventually it was borrowed to write the word for 'if', which happened to be pronounced in the same way.

In other words many Chinese characters consist of radical + phonetic, just as if we represented the past tense of the verb 'to see' with a picture of a saw as the phonetic side by side with a picture of an eye as a 'radical' to indicate that it was the word pronounced 'saw' which has something to do with the eye. The matter is further complicated by the fact that the phonetics indicate that the words were homophones or near-homophones at the time when the radicals were introduced. Pronunciations have, of course, changed since then, so there are now groups of characters which share the same phonetic, but are pronounced very differently, e.g. *kung* 功 'achievement' (with the 'strength' radical), *k'ung* 空 'hollow', 'empty' (with the 'hole' radical), *chiang* 江 'river' (with the 'water' radical), and *hsiang* 項 'neck' (with the 'head' radical).

It is possible to divide Chinese characters up into the following categories in accordance with the principles underlying their composition:

A. SIMPLE CHARACTERS

(1) Simple pictographs, e.g. *tzu* 子 'child'.

(2) Indicators, e.g. *shang* 上 'above' and *hsia* 下 'below', a small class of characters in which the meaning is indicated diagrammatically rather than portrayed pictorially.

(3) Pictographs used to represent a related abstract meaning, e.g. *chiao* 交, originally a pictograph of a man with legs crossed, is used to mean 'exchange', 'contact', 'communicate with', etc.

(4) Pictographs loaned and used for a word of similar pronunciation, e.g. *lai* 來, originally meaning 'wheat', is used to write *lai* 'to come'.

B. COMPOUND CHARACTERS

(5) Compound pictographs, e.g. *hao* 好 'love' (consisting of pictographs of woman and child). These characters derive their meaning from the combination of the two ideas represented by the pictographs of which they are comprised.

(6) Radical + phonetic, e.g. *chiang* 江 'river'.

Having discussed the writing and pronunciation of the characters we must say something in general about their meaning. Although certain compound words exist in ancient Chinese, basically there is a one-to-one relationship between the Chinese character and the English word as it appears in the dictionary. The first point to notice about the word represented by the Chinese character is that it always remains the same and is never modified with affixes indicating case, tense, etc. When it is seen in isolation there is no formal indication what part of speech it is (such as is provided for in other languages by such phenomena as articles, etc.) and, given that it is functioning as a noun, there is no formal distinction between singular and plural, and, given that it is functioning as a verb, there is no formal distinction in regard to person, number, tense, mood, or voice. It is only when these words are strung together that they form a pattern enabling the reader to see from their juxtaposition which words are functioning as nouns, which as verbs, and which as adjectives, etc.

This is a situation which seems very strange to a Frenchman or a German, for the words which they use are subject to a great deal of variation; but it seems much less odd to the English, who dispense with nearly all of the paraphernalia of the highly inflected languages. Classical Chinese carries this process to the ultimate extreme, so that the relationship between words is never indicated by changes in their form, but solely by their order and meaning.

We can get some idea how this works by imagining what it would be like if English worked in the same way. Take a sentence in our sinicized English, 'Winter king head army march battle', and try to convert it into proper English. There seems to be no close relationship between the first two words, so 'winter' must be on its own, setting the time of the sentence—'in winter'. The next three words all generally function as nouns but in the present context look as if they must be subject-verb-object: the verb should probably go into the past tense because of the 'in winter', and the two nouns in the singular as there is no positive evidence that they should be taken as plural—'in winter the king headed his army'. The last two words, in this context and by parallelism with 'head army', must surely be 'and marched into battle', although in other contexts 'march' might be the month and 'Battle' the place-name. It is from the accumulation of evidence of this sort, generally applied unconsciously and automatically that one converts the row of uncommitted Chinese characters into an English sentence in which some of the words are formally committed to definite parts of speech by the presence of inflections, prepositions, articles, etc. It will be seen that indications of tense and number are not so indispensible as it may seem to those who are brought up to regard them as essential ingredients in the form of the verb. The difference of approach between English and Chinese is that English has to express tense and number whether it is relevant or not, whereas Chinese only expresses the time of an action when this is not otherwise clear from the context, and only expresses number when it is necessary and relevant to do so—and this it can do perfectly well by the use of specific numbers or by words meaning 'some', 'many', 'all', etc.

Some people have felt that, since there is no formal distinction between parts of speech in Chinese and the Chinese themselves have not traditionally made such distinctions, it is wrong for the European to impose these categories on the language. Thus it is wrong to call *wang* 王 'king' a noun because there is nothing formally to indicate that it is a noun and in certain contexts it functions as a verb meaning 'to reign' or as an adjective meaning 'royal' or 'kingly'. The most we can say is that it is functioning as a noun in a given context. But this is also true of the word 'king' even in English: if we say that king is a noun we are merely saying that it functions as a noun in a given context or that it functions as a noun in the majority of contexts; and obviously there are countless words which would better exemplify this point, e.g. 'down', which may function as noun, adjective, verb, adverb, or preposition. I shall therefore apply terms for various parts of speech to Chinese without hesitation, for it will be found convenient to do so for purposes of exposition. A further point to remember here is that, although there is nothing formally to prevent a Chinese word from functioning as any part of speech, and there are many which embrace the functions of noun, adjective, verb, and adverb quite freely, e.g. *jen* 仁 'humane', 'humaneness', 'humanely', 'to be humane', nevertheless because of their meaning many words will obviously have a very limited range of function. Further discussion of this point must be left to a later stage, when the student has acquired some knowledge of the language (see note 316).

Some scholars have felt that to apply European categories of any kind in the analysis of a language so different as Chinese was to run the risk of distorting the material, and that the scientific way of analysing such a language is to use only categories deducible from the material itself. But the necessary degree of detachment from one's own language is very difficult for the scholar to attain, and, if attained, is incommunicable to the average mind. Moreover it soon becomes obvious that such detachment is unnecessary, for Chinese behaves in much the same way as the other languages within one's experience. Many sentences are seen to be based on the subject-verb-object pattern, which is commonly encountered in other languages, nouns are qualified by adjectives, verbs are qualified by adverbs, and main clauses are qualified by subordinate clauses. After all, when we talk of the SVO (subject-verb-object) pattern, part of what we mean has to do with linguistic phenomena (word order, case endings, etc.) and part has to do with the external world—with the actor-action-goal of action relationship which is a part of our common experience inevitably reflected in the structure of languages. Similarly the adjective-noun relationship has to do not only with the structure of languages but also with the fact that things do have attributes. We can build gratefully on this common linguistic heritage, and make it our task to call attention to these correspondences between English and Chinese and to describe the Chinese language using terms which have become familiar to us in the learning of European languages, only introducing new terms and new concepts when there is some phenomenon which does not fit in with our previous linguistic experience. To build on our previous linguistic experience in this way, so that we can see how Chinese and English tackle similar linguistic situations in their different ways, teaches much about the genius of both languages and enriches rather than distorts our understanding of Chinese. Until any generally acceptable system of describing Classical Chinese is devised this is certainly the best policy.

It is obvious that in a language in which the words contain no formal indication of their relationship with other words, word-order is of great importance. The basic patterns are familiar in English, with the structure of the normal sentence following the subject-verb-object pattern, and with qualifier preceding what it qualifies, i.e. adjectives preceding nouns and adverbs preceding verbs. Nevertheless there is, as we shall see, considerable scope for departing from this basic pattern for the sake of emphasis, clarity, or balance.

Apart from learning such simple rules of word order, the main task, as I said at the beginning, is to learn the function and meanings of various grammatical words. There is no need to hold the reader back any longer from this occupation.

GUIDE TO PRONUNCIATION

Initial consonants are pronounced approximately as in English, except for:

ch	like a soft 'g', as in 'gin'.
ch'	like 'ch', as in 'chin'.
hs	somewhat like 'sh', but more like 'ch' in German 'ich'.
j	somewhat like an initial 'r', as in 'run'.
k	like a hard 'g' as in 'gun'.
k'	like 'k', as in 'keep'.
p	like 'b', as in 'bun'.
p'	like 'p', as in 'pun'.
t	like 'd', as in 'don'.
t'	like 't', as in 'ton'.
ts or tz	like 'dz', as in 'adze'.
ts' or tz'	like 'ts', as in 'Whitsun'.

Final consonants:

h	is unpronounced, and n and ng are approximately as in English. No other final consonants occur.

Vowels are pronounced as follows:

a	as in 'father'.
ai	as in 'Taiwan', i.e. like 'y' in 'my'.
ao	like 'ow' in 'cow'.
e	like 'ir' in 'sir', *but* after 'y' it is pronounced as in 'yes'.
	en is like 'un' in 'fun'.
	eng is like 'ung' in 'dung'.
	erh is like 'urr' in 'furry'.
	ei is as in 'feint'.
i	like 'ee' in 'bee' *but* before another vowel it is shortened as in 'piano'.
	in is as in 'tin'.
	ih is a cross between the 'ir' in 'sir' and the 'oo' in 'good'.
o	after h, k, and k' like 'er' in 'her'.
	after all other consonants like 'aw' in 'law'.
ou	like 'owe'.
u	like 'oo' in 'good' *but* after ss, tz, tz' it is virtually silent.
	after y it is pronounced like 'owe'.
	ua is as in 'suave'.
	ui and uei are pronounced 'way'.
	uo is pronounced 'war'.
ü	like 'u' in French 'tu'.

9

NOTE ON PUNCTUATION

ALTHOUGH old Chinese texts were either completely unpunctuated or punctuated only with dots to indicate pauses in the reading, systems of punctuation akin to our own have been adopted in modern times. Many books are now published with the text running from left to right in horizontal lines, and it is possible for our system of punctuation to be adopted in its entirety; but for texts printed in vertical columns this is not completely possible. Instead of quotation marks ¬ occurs at the beginning of a quotation and ⌣ at the end. In some texts quotations within quotations are indicated by ¬ and ⌣, but I have omitted these signs. I have also dispensed with question marks and exclamation marks, although these also are sometimes used. Proper names are indicated by the presence of a vertical line at the left-hand side of the character or characters, and book titles are similarly indicated by means of a wavy line. The comma is used only to separate clauses: its function of marking off items in a list is taken over by a different mark (see between 21g and 21h).

KEY TO THE RADICALS OF
ALL THE CHARACTERS WHICH OCCUR
IN PASSAGE A

1a	孟	子	39	1w	乎	丿	4	3v	乘	丿	4
1b	子	子	39	1z	對	寸	41	3w	之	丶*	4
1c	見	見	147	2c	何	亻	9	3y	弒	弋	56
1d	梁	木	75	2d	必	心	61	3z	其	八	12
1e	惠	心	61	2i	仁	亻	9	4a	君	口	30
1f	王	王	96	2j	義	羊	123	4b	者	耂	125
1h	曰	曰	73	2l	已	己	49	4q	百	白	106
1i	叟	又	29	2m	矣	矢	111	4v	取	又	29
1j	不	一	1	2u	大	大	37	4x	馬	馬	86
1k	遠	辶	162	2v	夫	大	37	5d	為	爪	87
1l	千	十	24	3b	家	宀	40	5f	多	夕	36
1m	里	里	166	3c	士	士	33	5h	苟	艸	140
1n	而	而	126	3d	庶	广	53	5j	後	彳	60
1o	來	人	9	3e	人	人	9	5m	先	儿	10
1p	亦	亠	8	3k	身	身	158	5p	奪	大	37
1q	將	寸	41	3l	上	一	1	5r	饜	食	184
1r	有	月	74	3m	下	一	1	5s	未	木	75
1s	以	人	9	3n	交	亠	8	5w	遺	辶	162
1t	利	刂	18	3o	爭	爪	87	5y	親	見	147
1u	吾	口	30	3s	危	卩	26	6a	也	乚	5
1v	國	囗	31	3u	萬	艸	140				

* This character is surprisingly classified under Radical 4, although no part of it looks like that radical.

B   A

孟子見梁惠王王

曰「王何必曰利亦有仁義而已矣王曰何以利吾國大夫曰何以利其

吾家士庶人曰何以利吾身上下交爭利而國危矣萬乘之國弒其

君者必千乘之家千乘之國弒其君者必百乘之家萬取千焉千取

百焉不為不多矣苟為後義而先利不奪不饜未有仁而遺其親者

也未有義而後其君者也王亦曰仁義而已矣何必曰利」

梁惠王曰：「寡人之於國也盡心焉耳矣河內凶則移其民於河東移

其粟於河內河東凶亦然察鄰國之政無如寡人之用心者鄰國之

民不加少寡人之民不加多何也」孟子對曰「王好戰請以戰喻填然

鼓之兵刃既接棄甲曳兵而走或百步而後止或五十步而後止以

五十步笑百步則何如」曰：「不可直不百步耳是亦走也」曰：「王如知此

則無望民之多於鄰國也不違農時穀不可勝食也數罟不入洿池

C

24　23　22　21　20　19　18　17　16　15　14　13

a b c d e f g h i j k l m n o p q r s t u v w x y z

13 魚鼈不可勝食也;斧斤以時入山林,材木不可勝用也.穀與魚鼈不

14 可勝食,材木不可勝用,是使民養生喪死無憾也.養生喪死無憾,王

15 道之始也.五畝之宅,樹之以桑,五十者可以衣帛矣.雞豚狗彘之畜,

16 無失其時,七十者可以食肉矣.百畝之田,勿奪其時,數口之家可以

17 無饑矣.謹庠序之教,申之以孝悌之義,頒白者不負戴於道路矣.七

18 十者衣帛食肉,黎民不饑不寒,然而不王者,未之有也.狗彘食人食

19 而不知檢,塗有餓莩而不知發;人死,則曰:非我也,歲也.是何異於刺

20 人而殺之,曰:非我也,兵也.王無罪歲,斯天下之民至焉」

21 齊宣王問曰:「齊桓、晉文之事可得聞乎」孟子對曰:「仲尼之徒無道桓、

22 文之事者,是以後世無傳焉,臣未之聞也.無以,則王乎」曰:「德何如則

23 可以王矣」曰:「保民而王,莫之能禦也」曰:「若寡人者,可以保民乎哉」曰:

24 「可」曰:「何由知吾可也」曰:「臣聞之.胡齕曰,王坐於堂上,有牽牛而過堂

D

25 下者，王見之，曰：牛何之[84]？對曰：將以釁鐘[85]。王曰：舍之，吾不忍其觳觫若[86]

26 無罪而就死地。對曰：然則廢釁鐘與[87]？曰：何可廢也。以羊易之，不識有

27 諸[88]？曰：有之[89]。是心足以王矣[89]，百姓皆以王為愛也[90]，臣固知王之不忍

28 也[91]。王曰：然誠有百姓者[92]。齊國雖褊小，吾何愛一牛。即不忍其觳觫若[94]

29 無罪而就死地[95]，故以羊易之也[98]。曰：王無異於百姓之以王為愛也。以

30 小易大，彼惡知之[96][97]。王若隱其無罪而就死地[101]，則牛羊何擇焉[99]？王笑曰：

31 是誠何心哉[100]，我非愛其財而易之以羊也[102]。宜乎百姓之謂我愛也[105]。

32 無傷也，是乃仁術也[103]，見牛未見羊也[106][106]。君子之於禽獸也[104]，見其生[105]，不忍

33 見其死[105]，聞其聲，不忍食其肉。是以君子遠庖廚也。

34 魯平公將出，嬖人臧倉者請曰[107]：他日君出，則必命有司所之[108][108][109]。今乘輿[110]

35 已駕矣[111]，有司未知所之，敢請[114]。公曰：將見孟子。曰：何哉，君所為輕身以[113]

36 先於四夫者，以為賢乎[114]。禮義由賢者出[115]；而孟子之後喪踰前喪。君無

a
b
c
d
e
f
g
h
i
j
k
l
m
n
o
p
q
r
s
t
u
v
w
x
y
z

E

37　見馬」[116]公曰：「諾」樂正子入見[117]曰：「君奚為不見孟軻也」曰：「或告寡人曰，孟

38　子之後喪踰前喪[119]，是以不往見也」曰：「何哉君所謂踰者，前以士[118]後以

39　大夫；前以三鼎而後以五鼎與[120].」曰：「否[121]；謂棺椁衣衾之美也[122].

40　踰也.貧富不同也[123]」樂正子見孟子曰：「克[124]告於君君為來見也[125].嬖人有[126]

41　臧倉者沮君君是以不果來也[127]」曰：「行[128]或使之；止或尼之[128].行止非人所[129]

42　能也.吾之不遇魯侯[130]，天也.臧氏之子焉能使予不遇哉[131].

43　孟子將朝王王使人來曰：「寡人如就見者也[133]，有寒疾不可以風[134]朝，將[135]

44　視朝，不識可使寡人得見乎[135].」[136]對曰：「不幸而有疾[136]，不能造朝[137]」明日出弔[137]

45　於東郭氏.公孫丑[138]曰：「昔者辭以病[139]，今日弔，或者不可乎[141]」曰：「昔者疾，今[140]

46　日愈[138]，如之何不弔[138]」王使人問疾[139]，醫來.孟仲子[141]對曰：「昔者有王命，有采[140]

47　薪之憂[140]，不能造朝[142].今病小愈[142]，趨造於朝，我不識能至否乎[141]」使數人要[144]

48　於路[140]，曰：「請必無歸[142]而造於朝[143]」不得已[143]而之景丑氏宿焉.景子曰：「內則[144]

a b c d e f g h i j k l m n o p q r s t u v w x y z

15

F

60	59	58	57	56	55	54	53	52	51	50	49	

之患盛然後當一夫之戰，一夫之戰其不御三軍既可睹矣.翟以為

為得尺布，其不能煖天下之寒者既可睹矣.翟慮被堅執銳救諸侯

下之人矣.盛然後當一婦人之織，分諸天下，不能人得尺布，籍而以

而以為得一升粟，其不能飽天下之饑者既可睹矣.翟慮織而衣天

食天下之人矣.盛然後當一農之耕，分諸天下，不能人得一升粟.

以勞人有財以分人乎」吳慮曰「有.」子墨子曰「翟嘗計之矣.翟慮耕而

謂子墨子「義耳義耳，焉用言之哉.」子墨子曰「子之所謂義者，亦有力

魯之南鄙人有吳慮者，冬陶夏耕，自比於舜.子墨子聞而見之.吳慮

非堯舜之道，不敢以陳於王前，故齊人莫如我敬王也.」

義為不美也.其心曰「是何足與言仁義也」云爾，則不敬莫大乎是.我

未見所以敬王也」曰「惡是何言也.齊人無以仁義與王言者，豈以仁

父子外則君臣，人之大倫也.父子主恩，君臣主敬.丑見王之敬子也，

a b c d e f g h i j k l m n o p q r s t u v w x y z

16

G

| 72 | 71 | 70 | 69 | 68 | 67 | 66 | 65 | 64 | 63 | 62 | 61 |

不[176]若[176]誦先王之道而求其說，通聖人之言，以察其辭，[177]上說王、公、大人，次[177]匹夫、徒步之士。王、公、大人用吾言，國必治[178]，匹夫、徒步之士用吾言，行必脩。故翟以為[179]雖不耕而食饑，不織而衣寒，功賢於耕而食之、織而衣之者也。[180]吳慮謂子墨子曰：「義耳義耳，焉用言之哉」[181]子墨子曰：「籍設[180]而天下不知耕，教人耕，與不教人耕而獨耕者，其功孰多。」「教人耕者，其功多。」子墨子曰：「籍設而攻不義之國，鼓而使眾進戰，與不鼓而使眾進戰而獨進戰者，其功孰多。」[182]吳慮曰：「鼓而進眾者，其功多[184]。」子墨子曰：「天下匹夫、徒步之士少知義，[182]而教天下以義者，功亦多。何[184]故[185]弗言也。若得鼓而進於義，[186]則吾義豈不益進哉[187]。」

公輸盤[189]為楚造雲梯之械。成，將以攻宋。[188]子墨子聞之，起於齊，行十日[189]十[189]夜而至於郢，見公輸盤。公輸盤[190]曰：「夫子[191]何命焉為[191]」子墨子曰：「北方[192]有侮臣[192]，願藉子殺之。」公輸盤不說[193]。子墨子曰：「請獻十金。」公輸盤曰：「吾

a
b
c
d
e
f
g
h
i
j
k
l
m
n
o
p
q
r
s
t
u
v
w
x
y
z

H

84	83	82	81	80	79	78	77	76	75	74	73	

義固不殺人」子墨子起再拜曰：「請說之．吾從北方聞子為梯，將以攻

宋．宋何罪之有？荊國有餘於地而不足於民．殺所不足而爭所有餘

不可謂智；宋無罪而攻之，不可謂仁；知而不爭，不可謂忠；爭而不得

不可謂強；殺義不少而殺眾不可謂知類．」

孔子與柳下季為友，柳下季之弟名曰盜跖．盜跖從卒九千人，橫行

天下，侵暴諸侯，穴室摳戶，驅人牛馬，取人婦女，貪得忘親，不顧父母

兄弟，不祭先祖所過之邑，大國守城，小國入保，萬民苦之．孔子謂柳

下季曰「夫為人父者必能詔其子，為人兄者必能教其弟．若父不能

詔其子，兄不能教其弟，則无貴父子兄弟之親矣．今先生世之才士

也，弟為盜跖，為天下害，而弗能教也，丘竊為先生羞之．丘請為先生

往說之．」柳下季曰「先生言為人父者必能詔其子，為人兄者必能教

其弟；若子不聽父之詔，弟不受兄之教，雖今先生之辯將奈之何哉．

18

85　且距之為人也，心如涌泉，意如飄風，強足以距敵，辯足以飾非，順其 [218] [219] [219] [220]

86　心則喜；逆其心則怒，易辱人以言。先生必无往。」孔子不聽，顏回為御， [221] [222]

87　子貢為右，往見盜跖。盜跖乃方休卒徒大山之陽，膾人肝而餔之。孔 [223] [224] [225] [225]

88　子下車而前見謁者曰：「魯人孔丘，聞將軍高義，敬再拜謁者。」謁者入 [222] [226]

89　通，盜跖聞之大怒，目如明星，髮上指冠，曰：「此夫魯國之巧偽人孔丘 [227] [228] [229] [230]

90　非邪？為我告之：爾作言造語，妄稱文、武，冠枝木之冠，帶死牛之脅，多 [228] [229] [231] [231]

91　辭繆說，不耕而食，不織而衣，搖唇鼓舌，擅生是非，以迷天下之主，使 [231] [231]

92　天下學士不反其本，妄作孝悌，而徼倖於封侯富貴者也。子之罪大 [232]

93　極重，疾走不歸，我將以子肝益舖之膳。」孔子復通曰：「丘得幸於 [232] [232]

94　季，願望履幕下。」謁者復通盜跖曰：「使來前。」孔子趨而進，避席反走，再 [233] [234] [234]

95　拜盜跖。盜跖大怒，兩展其足，案劍瞋目，聲如乳虎，曰：「丘來前！若所言 [235] [234]

96　順吾意則生，逆吾心則死。」孔子曰：「丘聞之，凡天下有三德：生而長大， [235] [235] [236]

a
b
c
d
e
f
g
h
i
j
k
l
m
n
o
p
q
r
s
t
u
v
w
x
y
z

| 108 | 107 | 106 | 105 | 104 | 103 | 102 | 101 | 100 | 99 | 98 | 97 |

a
b
c
d
e
f
g
h
i
j
k
l
m
n
o
p
q
r
s
t
u
v
w
x
y
z

97: 美好无雙少長貴賤見而皆說之,此

98: 中德也;勇悍果敢聚衆率兵此下德也.凡人有此一德者,足以南面

99: 稱孤矣.今將軍兼此三者,身長八尺二寸面目有光脣如激丹齒如

100: 齊貝,音中黃鐘,而名曰盜跖.丘竊為將軍恥不取焉.將軍有意聽臣,

101: 臣請南使吳、越,北使齊、魯,東使宋、衞,西使晉、楚,使為將軍造大城數

102: 百里,立數十萬戶之邑,尊將軍為諸侯,與天下更始,罷兵休卒,收養

103: 昆弟,共祭先祖.此聖人才士之行,而天下之願也.」

104: 優施教驪姬夜半而泣謂公曰:「吾聞申生甚好仁而彊,甚寬惠而慈

105: 於民,皆有所行之.今謂君惑於我,我必亂國,無乃以國故而行彊於君,

106: 君未終命而不殘,君其若之何.盡殺我,無以一妾亂百姓」公曰:「夫豈

107: 惠其民而不惠於其父乎」驪姬曰:「妾亦懼矣.吾聞之,外人言曰:『為仁

108: 與為國不同.為仁者,愛親之謂仁;為國者,利國之謂仁.故長民者無

20

109　親，衆[263]以為親；苟利衆而百姓和，豈能憚君。以[264]衆故[264]不敢愛親，衆[265]況孰[267]厚

110　之。彼將惡始而美終，以晚蓋者也。凡[268]民利而生，殺君而厚利衆，衆悅其甚

111　沮之。殺親無惡於人，人孰去之。苟[269]交[269]利而得寵，志行而衆悅，欲其甚

112　矣，紂不惑焉。雖欲愛君，惑不釋也。今夫[269]以君為紂，若紂有良子，而先

113　喪，紂無章其惡而厚其敗；鈞之死也，無必假手於武王，而其世不廢

114　祀。至於今[270]吾豈知紂之善否[271]哉。君欲勿恤[272]其可乎[273]若大難至而恤之，

115　其[274]何及[274]矣。君懼[275]曰：「若何而可[275]」驪姬曰：「君盍老而授[276]之政，彼得政而行

116　其[277]欲得其所索[277]乃[278]為其釋君。且君其圖[279]之，自桓[280]叔以來，孰能愛親。唯無

117　親，故能兼翼。公曰：「不可與政。我以武與威，是以臨諸侯。未歿而亡政，[281]

118　不可謂武；有子而弗勝，不可謂威。我授之政，[282]諸侯必絕；能絕[283]於我，必

119　能害我。失政而害國，不可忍也。爾勿憂，吾將圖[282]之。」驪姬曰：「以[283]臯落狄

120　之朝夕苟我邊鄙，使無日以[283]牧田野，君之倉廩固不實，又[284]恐削封疆。

J

121. 君盍使之伐[286]狄，以觀其果[285]於眾也。與眾之信，輯睦[287]焉[288]。若不勝[289]狄，雖[289]濟[291]

122. 其罪可也。若勝狄，則善用眾矣[290]，求必益廣[287]，乃[288]可厚圖也。且夫勝[289]狄[289]，諸

123. 侯驚懼，吾邊鄙不儆，倉廩盈，四鄰服，封疆信，君得其賴；又知可否，其

124. 利多矣。君其圖之」公說[292]，是故使申生伐東山。

125. 晉侯[293]賞從亡者介[293]之推不言祿，祿亦弗及。推[294]曰：「獻公之子九人[294]，唯君

126. 在矣[295]。惠懷無親[299]，外內棄之[300]，天未絕[301]晉，必將有主[297]。主[297]晉祀者[304]，非君而誰[298]。其母

127. 天實置之[299]，而二三子以為己力[300]，不亦誣乎[301]。竊人之財[302]，猶謂之盜[303]，況[304][305][306]

128. 天之功以為己力乎[307]。下義其罪，上賞其姦，上下相蒙[305]，難與處[306]矣。

129. 曰：「盍亦求之以死[307]，誰懟[309]。」對曰「尤[310]而效之[310]，罪又甚焉。且出[311]怨言[311]，不食其

130. 食。」其母曰「亦使知之[312]，若何[310]」對曰「言[313]，身之[314]文也。身將[311]隱，焉用[311]文之，是求

131. 顯也[317]。」其母曰「能如是乎[315]，與女偕隱[316]。」遂隱而[316]死[316]。晉侯求之不獲，以縣上

132. 為之田[317]，曰：「以志吾過[318]，且旌善人」

K

142　141　140　139　138　137　136　135　134　133

133　九月甲午晉侯、秦伯圍鄭，以其無禮於晉，且貳於楚也。晉軍函陵，秦

134　軍汜南。佚之狐言於鄭伯曰：「國危矣，若使燭之武見秦君，師必退」公

135　從之。辭曰「臣之壯也，猶不如人；今老矣，無能為也已」公曰「吾不能早

136　用子，今急而求子，是寡人之過也。然鄭亡，子亦有不利焉」許之。夜縋

137　而出，見秦伯曰：「秦、晉圍鄭，鄭既知亡矣。若亡鄭而有益於君，敢以煩

138　執事。越國以鄙遠，君知其難也。焉用亡鄭以陪鄰？鄰之厚，君之薄也。

139　若舍鄭以為東道主，行李之往來，共其乏困，君亦無所害。且君嘗為

140　晉君賜矣，許君焦、瑕，朝濟而夕設版焉，君之所知也。夫晉何厭之有？

141　既東封鄭，又欲肆其西封。若不闕秦，將焉取之？闕秦以利晉，唯君圖

142　之」秦伯說，與鄭人盟。

a b c d e f g h i j k l m n o p q r s t u v w x y z

319　319　320　320　321　322　322　323　323　324　325　326　327　327　328　328　329　330　330　331　331　332　333　333　334　335　335　336　337　337　338　339　340

23

GRAMMATICAL NOTES

PASSAGE A

THIS is the opening chapter of the book of Mencius, and it deals with the first encounter between the philosopher and King Hui of Liang (also known as Wei), a state in the great bend of the Yellow River in central China. King Hui reigned from 370 to 319 B.C.

1.　　In this first sentence we have a straightforward SVO pattern. The other point to notice is that the more general terms *tzu* 子 'master' and *wang* 王 'king' are qualified, or determined, by the more specific proper names *Meng* 孟 and *Hui* 惠, the latter being further determined by the state-name *Liang* 梁. One can think of the word-order in such cases as answering a series of questions as one works from back to front: king—which king?—King Hui—which King Hui?—King Hui of Liang. The verb in this sentence must obviously be translated in the past tense.

2.　　The function word *erh* 而 is one of the most common words in ancient Chinese. In the great majority of cases it serves to separate two clauses. 'And' or 'but' is often a satisfactory translation, but since in the great majority of cases the clause preceding the *erh* 而 is in some sense subordinate to the one succeeding it, it is often better to render this relationship between the two clauses by translating the verb of the first clause in the appropriate participial form. Thus, in the present context, 'You come, not considering a thousand *li* too far'. Sometimes, when the nature of the subordination is clear from the context, it is permissible to introduce the subordinate clause by 'although', 'since', 'if' or some other appropriate word, just as two juxtaposed clauses, with no conjunction marking the relationship between them, may have a conditional relationship which is implicit in the context and which has to be made more explicit in translation (cf. notes 12 and 23 for instances of this). It should be noted that *erh* 而 does not *always* indicate that the clause preceding it is subordinate. Sometimes the clause preceding the *erh* 而 must be taken as the main clause, and the clause succeeding it as a consequence or purpose clause to be introduced by the words 'so that' or 'in order to'.

3.　　Since *erh* 而 is normally preceded by a clause we must look out for a verb. Here the presence of *pu* 不, which most commonly functions as the adverb which serves to negate verbs, immediately suggests that *yüan* 遠 may be the verb. The sense of *yüan* 遠—'far', 'remote'—is basically adjectival, but it may function as an intransitive verb—'to be far'. Sometimes verbs which one would normally expect to be intransitive since their sense does not require an object *do* take an object, and in these contexts such verbs are being used in a causative or putative sense. Thus *yüan* 遠 followed by an object means 'to cause to be far' or 'to regard as far': in the present context, '(you) do not regard-as-far a thousand *li*'.

24

4.   The basic meaning of *i* 亦 is 'also', but sometimes, as here, it is necessary to translate 'in view of this', 'therefore', 'in consequence'. In such cases the notion of consequence is really already implicit in the relationship between the subject-matter of the clause containing the *i* 亦 and that of the one preceding it. So although an *i* 亦 merely implies that the subject matter of the second clause is an additional consideration and not a consequential one, an expresson implying consequence is often desirable in translation.

5.   *chiang* 將 is an auxiliary verb meaning 'to be about to'. It is the standard way of indicating the future in Mencius. It also means 'to lead', 'leader', 'general', 'admiral', but in this sense it is read in the fourth tone rather than in the first. It will be noticed that many other Chinese characters have more than one reading to indicate differences of meaning, some, like *chiang* 將, being read in different tones and some with entirely different pronunciations.

There are various words like *chiang* 將 which perform a function roughly analogous to the formation of tenses in English, but such words are used extremely rarely in comparison with their English equivalents. It is therefore best to avoid using such terms as 'tense' or 'aspect' in connection with them, since these terms are normally used for inalienable features of the verb in languages in which indication of tense or aspect is always present in the form of the verb. I prefer to call them 'temporal auxiliaries'.

6.   *i* 以 is another of the most common words in ancient Chinese. The basic idea common to all its meanings is that of 'instrumentality', and it has therefore been called by some writers the instrumental particle, but it has a wide variety of function. Occasionally it occurs as a noun in the sense of 'wherewithal', 'means', 'purpose'. As a verb it means 'to use', but its use as a main verb is not normal. The closely related use as a verb-preposition in the sense of 'using', 'by means of', 'according to' is however very common. Sometimes it acts as a link between two clauses in the sense of 'and thus', 'and thereby', and sometimes it introduces purpose clauses ('wherewith to', 'in order to') or causal clauses ('through', 'because of'). Here it is obviously the object of *yu* 有 'to have' and might be translated 'means' or 'wherewithal', but at the same time it provides a natural lead in to the purposive 'to profit my kingdom'.

7.   The final particle *hu* 乎 is the normal means of indicating a formal interrogative (the interrogative which expects the answer 'yes' or 'no', as contrasted with the material interrogative—who?, when?, why?, etc.—which demands new information). The word-order of the formal interrogative sentence is always the same as that of the cognate indicative sentence, i.e. the function of *hu* 乎 is rather like the 'won't you?' in 'you will have means to profit my kingdom, won't you?', and indeed this pattern may sometimes provide a better translation than the standard English interrogative pattern 'Will you have . . .?'

8.   *ho* 何 is the most common material interrogative. It may mean 'what?', 'why?', 'how?', or 'where?', and we shall find that it can play a variety of roles in a sentence. Here it occupies the adverbial position and means 'why?' We shall

shortly meet *ho i* 何以, 'by means of what?', 'how?', which is also very common. The inversion of preposition and interrogative in this expression is reminiscent of 'wherewith' and 'whereby' in English.

9.　　*yüeh* 曰 'said' is commonly used to introduce direct speech, and we have already met it twice in this capacity. Similarly here it indicates that the word *li* 利 'profit' is being quoted—'Why must you mention "profit"?'

Notice that the second person pronoun is comparatively rare in Classical Chinese, and people are commonly addressed in the third person. In other words, there is no difference between 'why must the king mention "profit"?' (the question being addressed to someone other than the king) and 'why must you, Your Majesty, mention "profit"?' Compare the use of *sou* 叟 in the first line.

10.　　Notice that Mencius takes the king up by repeating the *i yu* 亦有 which he has already used in *i chiang yu* 亦將有. This device clearly focuses attention on the repeated words, and in translation it seems necessary to adopt a wording which throws emphasis on them, e.g. 'What I have in view of this is benevolence and justice'.

11.　　*erh i i* 而已矣 (literally, 'and finish') means 'and that's all'. It is a common idiom which can often be rendered more smoothly in English by 'all (I have) is', '(I have) nothing but', '(I) only (have)', or some similar expression. Occasionally *erh i* 而已 is found with the same meaning.

It should be noted that there are two other characters which look very much like *i* 已, *viz. chi* 己 and *ssu* 巳. Some dictionaries are helpful in warning against the possibility of confusing characters which look alike.

12.　　From *wang yüeh* 王曰 to *erh kuo wei i* 而國危矣 may all be treated as one sentence. The construction does not become completely clear until one reaches the end. Then one sees that the *erh* 而 imposes a subordination on the preceding clause, which is clearly conditional in character—'if superiors and inferiors contend with each other for profit, then the state will be endangered'. Looking back to the earlier part of the sentence, one then sees a conditional relationship implicit in the earlier clauses—'if Your Majesty says . . ., then the grandees will say . . ., and the knights and the common people will say . . .'.

13.　　A clause terminated by the final particle *i* 矣 describes *either* an event or action which is taking place (or will take place) *once and for all,* or an event or action which has been completed. It does not describe a state or condition or a continuing action. Thus here the *kuo wei i* 國危矣 means 'the country will be endangered' or 'will be brought into danger', not 'will be in a state of danger'.

Notice that the natural translation of the verb here is in the future tense, but there is no need for a temporal auxiliary in the Chinese because the future is sufficiently implicit in the context and in the conditional relationship between the clauses.

14.　　Early forms of the graph *chiao* 交 show a man with legs crossed, and the word has a range of meanings to do with human relationships—'exchange', 'join', 'have relations with', 'meeting', etc. Its grammatical usage is as a pronominal adverb meaning 'with each other', 'mutually'.

Notice that there is no preposition after *cheng* 爭 whereas we need to say 'struggle for', 'contend over'. Prepositions occur rarely. *cheng* 爭 followed by a noun always does have the sense of 'to contend over' (never 'to contend with').

15. *chih* 之 is the most common word in late Chou Chinese literature. It has two principal functions: 1. as a third person pronoun which normally comes immediately after the verb and supplies its object ('him', 'her', 'it', 'them'); 2. as a possessive or determinative particle. In the phrase *Hui wang chih kuo* 惠王之國 'King Hui's state', it is clearly performing a possessive function, but in *wan ch'eng chih kuo* 萬乘之國 its function is determinative. It determines or limits the concept 'state' to 'state of ten thousand chariots'. 'State of ten thousand chariots' is a conventional way of referring to a major state.

16. The most common use of the function word *che* 者 is exemplified here. It converts a verbal sentence into a noun clause with the sense of 'he who . . .', 'those who . . .'. Thus here the addition of *che* 者 turns 'he assassinates its ruler' into 'he who assassinates its ruler'. It might be termed the substantivizing particle.

17. *ch'i* 其 is normally a third person possessive pronoun—'his', 'her', 'its', 'their'. (The graph is also used to write an auxiliary verb which is common in certain authors, but this does not concern us here). Its use in this sentence is to be carefully noted. The proper translation of this *che*-clause is 'He who assassinates' the ruler of a state of ten thousand chariots', but the Chinese avoids the clumsiness of three nouns being linked by two *chih*'s 之 or 'ofs' by saying 'state of ten thousand chariots, he who assassinates its ruler'. This device also has the effect of emphasizing an element in the sentence by placing it at the beginning, with the *ch'i* 其 serving to indicate where this element would go in a normal unemphatic word-order. This use of *ch'i* 其 is a common feature of the language.

18. *pi* 必 is usually an auxiliary verb meaning 'must', but sometimes it is more satisfactory to translate it adverbially in the sense of 'always', 'invariably', 'inevitably'. This illustrates the difficulty of rigid analysis in Indo-European terms, for there is no formal distinction between passages in which it is translated as an auxiliary verb and those in which it is translated as an adverb, and in both cases the word after *pi* 必 functions as a verb. Here, however, *pi* 必 occurs as a main verb with the sense 'destined for', 'bound to become'. This is not very common.

19. *yen* 焉 may be regarded as standing for *yü chih* 於之 'from it', 'to it', 'in it', 'than it', 'by it' (*yü* 於 is a multipurpose preposition which will call for further discussion when we meet it later, see note 47. On *chih* 之 see note 15). Instead of the natural word-order 'to take a thousand from ten thousand' the Chinese says 'ten thousand—to take a thousand from it'. This is a useful device because it means that the *wan* 萬 'ten thousand' and *ch'ien* 千 'a thousand' retain the initial positions occupied in the previous sentences. They derive emphasis from this, and the whole passage gains in balance and clarity. In fact

both *yen* 焉 and the pronoun *chih* 之 are frequently used with the same effect as the usage of *ch'i* 其 described in note 17, viz. to place at the front of the sentence an important element which is not the grammatical subject of the sentence. (For an example of *chih* 之 used in this way see note 53.)

Note that, although *yen* 焉 clearly stands for *yü chih* 於之, this does not mean that it is a phonetic fusion of the two words. It is probably a fusion of *yü* 於 with an obsolete pronoun pronounced with final -n. The phenomenon of phonetic fusion of two commonly juxtaposed words is familiar enough in English: e.g. 'won't' is a phonetic fusion of 'will not'. Naturally when this same process happened in the spoken language of ancient China a single character seemed sufficient to represent the word resulting from the fusion. About a dozen fusion words like *yen* 焉 have now been identified with certainty, and other instances of this phenomenon may yet be detected. For the study of phonetic fusions a knowledge of the hypothetical reconstructions of the pronunciations of Chinese words in antiquity is obviously necessary; but this is a large topic which it is not necessary for the beginner to study, so it has been avoided in the preparation of this book.

yen 焉 is also used as an interrogative adverb (see note 131).

20.   *pu* 不 is the commonest negative in ancient Chinese. It is a pure negative and has no positive antonym. Its two usages are both exemplified in this clause: 1. As we have already seen (cf. note 3), it negates verbs, as in *pu wei* 不為 'would not seem', compared with *wei* 為 'would seem' (the 'would' here being required by context); 2. With nouns and adjectives it performs the same function as a privative prefix (e.g. 'in-', 'un-') in European languages, as in *pu jen* 不仁 'inhumane', 'inhumanity' and *pu to* 不多 'not much', 'few', 'small'. Note that the meaning and function of *pu* 不 in these two usages is not really different. It is the nominalization of *jen* 仁 imposed by the sentence-pattern which makes it necessary to translate *pu jen* 不仁 as 'inhumanity' rather than 'is not humane': the function of *pu* 不 is always simply to negate.

21.   The verb *wei* 為 presents some difficulty and its range of meaning should be clearly understood. It means basically 'to do', 'to make', and in the passive therefore 'to be made', and so 'to become', 'to be'. (It should be remembered that verbs are neutral in respect of voice, and it is only the presence of an object after the verb which makes that verb clearly active.) But just as our word 'make' can apply to mental as well as physical acts (e.g. What do you make of it?), so *wei* 為 has another chain of meaning: 'to make out to be', 'to regard as', which in the passive becomes 'to be regarded as', 'to be reputed to', 'to seem'. Both the present instances of *wei* 為 come in the latter category. The sentence in which the second instance occurs should be translated: 'If you are reputed to put justice last and profit first'. Translators have missed the significance of this *wei* 為 and taken it as if it went with the *hou* 後 to mean '*regard* as last', 'put last', but all this is already implicit in the *hou* 後 when it is used as a verb, just as the *hsien* 先 which comes parallel with it means 'to put first' (cf. *yüan* 遠 'to regard as far', discussed in note 3).

GRAMMATICAL NOTES

22.   Notice that the subject of the *wei* 為 in *pu wei pu to* 不為不多 is a substantival clause with the *ch'ü* 取 acting like the English infinitive 'to take'. The final particle *i* 矣 at the end of this sentence indicates that it is not conceived as a vague generalization but as a real and urgent possibility.

23.   The sentence from *kou* 苟 to *yen* 饜 is conditional, with the protasis being introduced by *kou* 苟 meaning 'if'. But the apodosis, *pu to pu yen* 不奪不饜 is obviously a conditional sentence in itself: 'they will not be satisfied unless they are helping themselves'. We have already had a case of two juxtaposed clauses without conjunctions having an obvious conditional relationship (see note 12), and in a brief sentence like this words meaning 'if' or 'then' would seem to intrude unnecessarily, spoiling the balance of the sentence. This kind of construction persists in English expressions like 'no names, no pack-drill', and 'more haste, less speed'.

24.   Like *pu* 不, *wei* 未 is a pure negative, having no positive antonym, but unlike *pu* 不 which is weak and takes its degree of generality or particularity from the context, *wei* 未 negates absolutely and means 'never' or sometimes 'not yet'. The 'never' may be temporal ('it never has happened'), or logical ('it never happens', 'it never could happen') as here: 'there never exists one who, being humane, abandons his parents', i.e. such a thing is by definition impossible.

25.   The final particle *i* 矣 never occurs in conjunction with *wei* 未. This is understandable since *wei* 未 implies a generality which is alien to *i* 矣, which is appropriate to sentences describing something happening once and for all; while if the context is in the past *i* 矣 indicates that the action of the verb is completed and *wei* 未 that it is 'not yet' completed. *yeh* 也, which occurs here as a final particle, is more appropriate to sentences which express generalizations rather than deal with the particular and to those which express judgments or describe states, rather than narrate events or give commands.

   Notice the parallelism between this and the succeeding sentence. It will already be apparent that this is a common stylistic feature of the language.

26.   The construction *yu*—clause(s)—*che* 有 . . . 者 means 'there is one/are those who . . .'. The *jen* 仁 therefore stands on its own before the *erh* 而 as a separate clause and must consequently be taken, not as a noun ('humanity') or an adjective ('humane'), but as a verb meaning 'being humane' or, making more explicit the concessive nature of the clause, 'although he is humane'.

27.   Note that only the context tells the reader that this *yüeh* 曰 is imperative rather than indicative. In a negative imperative sentence the presence of negative imperative adverbs (q.v. note 57) will make it clear that the sentence is imperative rather than indicative, but in a positive imperative sentence there is no formal indication that the sentence is imperative rather than indicative.

PASSAGE B

MENCIUS attacks King Hui for neglecting the people and proposes measures for the improvement of their welfare (*Mencius* 1a. 3).

29

28.　　Instead of using the first person pronoun kings commonly refer to themselves as *kua-jen* 寡人 'the solitary person', but it is best simply to translate 'I'.
　　The construction of the sentence in which this phrase occurs is complicated. It is a permutation of the basic statement *kua-jen chin hsin yü kuo* 寡人盡心 於國 'I devote my mind to the state'. In order to lay emphasis on *kua-jen* 寡人 and *kuo* 國 these two elements are related to each other by appropriate function words and marked off from the rest of the sentence by means of the particle *yeh* 也—'as for *my* attitude towards the *state*' (literally, 'my towards the state', but one has to put a word like 'attitude' in to make sense in English). The *yü kuo* 於國 is later resumed by the particle *yen* 焉—'I devote my mind *to it*'. Notice the new use of *yeh* 也. When *yeh* 也 is not a final particle, it often marks off at the beginning of the sentence a psychological subject, an element or elements in the sentence which there is to be a statement about, but which would not form the grammatical subject if the statement were put in its simplest form.

29.　　*erh* 耳, which also means 'ear', is here used to write a phonetic fusion of *erh i* 而已 'and that's that'. As we have noticed before, the finality of the statement is often additionally emphasized by the presence of *i* 矣.

30.　　*tse* 則 'then' is a very common function word, coming between subordinate clause and main clause. Generally, as here, there is no function word introducing the subordinate clause. *tse* 則 may occasionally indicate a temporal or causal relationship between the clauses, but it is almost always safe to take the relationship as conditional. In the present context 'if', 'when', or 'whenever' would serve equally well to introduce the subordinate clause in the translation.
　　The word also occurs as a noun, meaning 'pattern', 'exemplar', 'model' and as a verb, 'to model oneself on'.

31.　　*jan* 然 here functions as a main verb with the sense of 'to be so' or 'to do so'. This is fairly uncommon, and it generally appears as a grammatical word, either (1) as substitute for a subordinate clause, with the meaning 'this being so'; in this proclausal usage it is often followed by *tse* 則 'then'; or (2) as an adverbial suffix equal to our '-ly'. It may also appear as a one-word answer to a question, meaning 'quite so', 'yes'. It is obviously the equivalent of *ju chih* 如之, 'to be like this' or 'to do like this', and is evidently a phonetic fusion of *ju* 如 with a certain obsolete and unidentified pronoun with a final -n (cf. *yen* 焉 note 19). (The word *ju* 如 is met for the first time in the next sentence of the text.)

32.　　*wu* 無 is the negative antonym of *yu* 有 'to have', 'there is', 'there are': it means 'to lack', 'there is not', 'there are not', 'lacking', 'without'. When it precedes a clause terminated by *che* 者, the construction means 'there is/are none who/which . . .' (cf. note 26 for the *yu*—clause—*che* 有 . . . 者 construction). Thus the text literally means 'there are none which resemble my using mind', i.e. 'there are none which resemble me in devotion'.

33.　　*chia shao* 加少, literally 'increasingly to become few', serves as a comparative verb, meaning 'to become fewer'.

34.　　Here we meet our first example of a very important usage of *yeh* 也. Apart from the ordinary verbal sentence there is another form of sentence, which I shall call non-verbal, since it lacks a main verb. This is the equivalent of the English sentence in which two terms are joined by a copula, i.e. X is Y. The Chinese for this is 'X Y *yeh*'.

　　In this sentence the 'Y' term is the interrogative *ho* 何, here meaning 'why?' So the pattern of the sentence is 'X *ho yeh*' X 何也, which is the equivalent of our 'Why is it that X?', the 'X' being a substantival clause or clauses. The two 'X' clauses *lin kuo chih min pu chia shao* 鄰國之民不加少 and *kua jen chih min pu chia to* 寡人之民不加多 would both need a possessive *chih* 之 after the *min* 民 to make them formally into substantival clauses ('my people's not increasing', cf. note 46), but it is a feature of the language that a possessive *chih* 之 drops out when it is in proximity to a more essential one.

35.　　Notice the abrupt change of subject here, the subject of *ch'ing* 請 being 'I' left unexpressed. If the context is understood, there is no real problem. As a rule one should assume that the same subject is retained throughout a passage until a new subject is expressed, unless, as here, the context makes it impossible.

36.　　Here we have a prepositional use of *i* 以—'by means of' (for *i* 以 see note 6).

37.　　Here is an instance of the use of *jan* 然 as an adverbial suffix (see note 31). *t'ien jan* 填然 means '*t'ien*-like', '*t'ien*-ly', i.e. 'with a noise which sounds like *t'ien*. *t'ien* 填 is here used not for its meaning, but for its sound, i.e. as an echoic word. 'Bang, bang' would be the English equivalent. The device of using words for their sound in this way has been used a good deal in Chinese, especially for the rendering of foreign technical terms or proper names. The whole clause means 'Bang, bang they drum it', i.e. 'Bang, bang go the drums'. This is our first use of *chih* 之 as the objective pronoun.

　　In ancient China drums were used to sound the advance into battle.

38.　　*chi* 既 is a common temporal auxiliary, serving to indicate that the action of the verb is completed. Here 'the weapon blades *having* clashed'.

39.　　Note the use of *huo* 或 . . . *huo* 或 . . . , 'some . . . , others . . .'.

40.　　*erh hou* 而後 is a common expression meaning 'and afterwards' or sometimes 'consequently'. The most natural translation here, as often, is 'before' with the present participle—'some ran fifty paces before stopping' (the word *tsou* 走 'ran', which was the last word in the previous sentence, is implicit here although left unexpressed). Sometimes, however, *erh hou* 而後 is used in exactly the same way as *jan hou* 然後, q.v. note 166.

41.　　Another example of the prepositional use of *i* 以—'through', 'because of'.

42.　　In the expression *ho ju* 何如 *ho* 何 is the interrogative pronoun object of the verb *ju* 如 'to be like', 'to do like', with no subject expressed. It means 'what is it like?' and is commonly used in the sense of 'what would that be like?' or 'what would you think of that?'

43.　　*shih i tsou yeh* 是亦走也 'this too is running away' is an example of a simple non-verbal (XY 也 = X is Y) type of sentence, *tsou* 走 here functioning not as a verb, but as a noun. In this construction the *i* 亦 always attaches to the subject: *shih i tsou yeh* could not mean 'this is also running away (besides being other things)'.

44.　　*ju* 如 here means 'if'. In almost all cases it follows the subject of the 'if' clause. It gives a remote flavour to the condition—'if Your Majesty were to understand this, then you would be without expectation that. . . .' We have already met *ju* 如 in the sense of 'to be like', 'to do like' (cf. notes 31 and 42), and there seems to be an affinity between the two meanings, since 'if' means 'in a situation like', 'in such a situation that'.

45.　　Here we have two words for 'this' coming in quick succession, *shih* 是 and *tz'u* 此. The difference between them is that when there is a contrast between 'this' and 'that' *tz'u* 此 is used in contrast with *pi* 彼 'that' (cf. note 96). *shih* 是, on the other hand, is 'what we have just been talking about', 'the afore-mentioned', and 'that' may sometimes be as suitable a translation as 'this'.

46.　　*min chih to yü lin kuo yeh* 民之多於鄰國也, literally 'people's becoming more numerous than neighbouring states', is the equivalent of a that-clause in English after verbs of saying, knowing, etc. Thus the meaning is 'that the people will become more numerous than (those of) neighbouring states'. The *yeh* 也 is part of the formula as well as the possessive *chih* 之, but is is sometimes omitted.

47.　　Note the use of *yü* 於 in the sense of 'than': it makes it necessary to translate the verb or adjective which precedes it in the comparative—'become more numerous'. We have already had *yü* 於 several times in this passage meaning 'to', 'towards', and in note 19 we noticed the meaning 'from'. Other meanings of this multipurpose preposition are 'in' and 'on', and it is also used to mean 'by', introducing the agent after a passive verb.

48.　　Chinese often uses an active construction with no subject expressed, where we would more naturally use a passive construction. The clause *pu wei nung shih* 不違農時 is an example of this. We would say: 'if the farming seasons are not disregarded'. In the present context the subsequent clauses parallel with this one all have subjects, so, in a language as rigidly parallelistic as this, the word-order for the subjectless clause must be the same as that of the subsequent clauses which have subjects.

　　Commencing here there is also a good example of a series of juxtaposed clauses whose conditional relationship is deduced from the context and not indicated by grammatical words (cf. note 23).

49.　　*pu k'o sheng* 不可勝 'cannot fully', 'cannot exhaustively' followed by a verb is a common idiom. Here 'the grain cannot exhaustively be eaten', i.e. 'there will be more than enough grain to eat'.

50.　　*wu-ch'ih* 洿池 is an example of the kind of reiterative compound word which is met occasionally in ancient Chinese and later becomes a very common feature of the language. The two elements have very similar meaning and one word will suffice in translation. *fu-chin* 斧斤 and *ts'ai-mu* 材木 in the next sentence are other examples.

51.　　As we have seen in the preceding sentences nouns do not normally need a word for 'and' to link them. Here we have *yü* 與 fulfilling this function. It is necessary here because it links two separate groups rather than two nouns of similar meaning. It also helps to preserve the series of two-character and four-character groupings which are typical of the language.

52.　　The *wu* 無 here should be treated as the main verb—'this will ensure that the people, both in their care of the living and in their mourning for the dead, will *be without* bitterness'. Since the qualifier precedes what it qualifies, the rules of word-order are against the interpretation of those translators who take *wu han* 無憾 as an adverbial expression—'without resentment'—qualifying the verbs *yang* 養 and *sang* 喪. Notice how this clause is repeated without alteration to become the subject of a non-verbal sentence (the 'X' of an 'X Y yeh' sentence) immediately afterwards.

53.　　The word order of *wu mou chih chai, shu chih i sang* 五畝之宅, 樹之以桑 should be carefully noticed. The 'natural' word order would be *i sang shu wu mou chih chai* 以桑樹五畝之宅 but by the device of the anaphoric use of the pronoun *chih* 之 (cf. note 19), the following advantages are gained: 1. The required emphasis is thrown on the *wu mou chih chai* 五畝之宅 which (although, in the 'natural' word-order, it would be the grammatical object) is the psychological subject of the sentence; 2. emphasis is also placed on the expression *i sang* 以桑 'with mulberry trees' because contrary to the 'natural' rule that the adverbial phrase should precede the verb since it qualifies it, it comes after the verb and thus assumes the kind of emphasis which one might render by treating *i* 以 as the main verb—'in planting them use *mulberry trees* (rather than any other kind of tree)'; 3. the neat four-character pattern is preserved.

　　The verb *shu* 樹 has to be taken as imperative rather than indicative. We do not know this for certain until we see that it is paralleled by verbs prefaced by the negative imperative adverbs discussed in note 57 (cf. note 27).

54.　　By extension of its usage with verbs *che* 者 is sometimes used with a non-verbal word or phrase to indicate a class of people. Thus *wu shih che* 五十者 means 'fifty-year-olds', and *pan pai che* 斑白者, which comes later in this passage, means 'grey-haired people'.

55.　　*k'o* 可 is a very common auxiliary verb indicating possibility in the widest sense. 'May' or 'can' is the usual translation. The important point which may be observed from comparing the examples in this passage is that, whereas *k'o* 可 by itself goes with passive verbs, with active verbs one always finds *k'o i* 可以 (as here) with no difference in meaning. (Active and passive verbs are, of course, formally distinguished by the existence or non-existence of an object after them.) Clauses with *k'o* 可 + passive verb are normally terminated with *yeh* 也. This is because the *k'o* 可 goes very closely with the verb to form the equivalent of an English adjective with -ble ending, e.g. *pu k'o yung yeh* 不可用 也 means 'is unusable'. The construction is thus of the non-verbal type, as, for example, in the passage discussed in note 49.

56.　　The use of the possessive pronoun *ch'i* 其 serves a similar purpose to the use of *chih* 之 described in note 53. Cf. also the use of *ch'i* 其 described in note 17.

57.　　Here we have two different negative imperative adverbs. The first is in many texts written 母, but in the text of Mencius it is misleadingly written in the same way as the much commoner *wu* 無 meaning 'to lack'. Sometimes it is difficult to decide in which sense the word should be taken. For example, the *wu* 無 in the passage quoted in note 44 might be taken as the negative imperative adverb ('do not expect') were it not that the presence of the *ju* 如 (making the condition remote) and of the *yeh* 也 (which is not to be expected in an imperative sentence) shows that that interpretation would be false.

There is a theory that 勿 = 母之, and this satisfactorily explains why the two different negative imperatives are used here. In the first case the verb *shih* 失 only takes one object—'do not neglect the *seasons*', but the verb *to* 奪 takes two objects—'do not deprive *them* of the *seasons* (i.e. of their seasonal labours)'. The 'them' (*chih* 之) is subsumed under the 勿. It is quite normal for the third person pronoun object *chih* 之 to precede the verb after a negative adverb (cf. note 59).

58.　　Notice that *pu . . . pu . . .* 不 . . . 不 . . . serves where we would have 'neither . . . nor . . .'.

59.　　*jan erh pu wang che, wei chih yu yeh* 然而不王者, 未之有也 is a common formula in Mencius. It means 'one who behaves like this is bound to become king'. *jan* 然 'if he behaves like this' forms a conditional clause summing up the ideal measures Mencius proposes that the king should adopt. *wang* 王 here functions as a verb—'to reign', so *pu wang che* 不王者 means 'one who does not reign'. ('To reign' in Mencius means to become ruler of all the Chinese states as a result of one's kingly virtues, to become a true king by behaving as a true king. King Hui and the other so-called kings of the states had usurped the title, which properly only belonged to the successors of the founder of the Chou Dynasty, who had long since lost their authoritative position.) *wei chih yu yeh* 未之有也 can best be understood by comparison with *wei yu* 未有 (see notes 24 and 26). In the passage to which these notes refer the *wei yu* 未有 came at the beginning of the sentence, but the sentence could be rewritten *jen erh i ch'i ch'in che, wei chih yu yeh* 仁而遺其親者, 未之有也, with the *chih* 之 referring back to the whole of the *che* 者 clause. So literally the idiom means 'There never exists one who does not reign as a king if he behaves like this', i.e. 'one who behaves like this is bound to reign as a king'.

Another interpretation of this idiom is possible, but it depends on a usage of *che* 者 which we have not met before. Apart from meaning 'one who does not reign', *pu wang che* 不王者 can mean 'the fact of not reigning', i.e. it may simply turn the *pu wang* 不王 into a substantival clause without personal reference. The translation would then be: 'in such circumstances failure to reign never happens'. This interpretation fits the *jan* 然 rather better since it can be taken as simply summing up the two previous clauses. Nevertheless the use of *che* 者 to form an impersonal substantival clause like this is quite rare. Moreover in dealing with ancient Chinese as with other ancient languages it is always advisable to plump for the concrete rather than the abstract interpretation where possible, so I prefer to take *pu wang che* 不王者 as 'one who does not reign', which will fit all the contexts in Mencius in which this idiom occurs.

In the *wei chih yu yeh* 未之有也 idiom the *chih* 之 precedes the verb after a negative adverb. This construction, which has already been mentioned in note 57, is quite normal, and other personal pronouns also occur as pre-verbal objects in negative sentences. For *yu chih* 有之 meaning 'it exists' or 'he exists', cf. note 88.

60.   Notice the construction after the verb *chih* 知 'to know'. We would have to say 'you do not understand *that you should* introduce restrictions', but the Chinese simply says 'you do not understand to restrict'. Notice again the change of subject from 'dogs and pigs' to 'you' without indication (cf. note 35).

61.   *fei* 非 is the negative appropriate to non-verbal sentences. 'X *fei* Y *yeh*' X 非 Y 也 means 'X is not Y'. It also sometimes negates verbal sentences, but with much more emphasis than *pu* 不. In such contexts it means 'it is not the case that', i.e. it does not simply negate the verb, but rejects the whole sentence.

62.   In *wo* 我 we have the form of first person pronoun which may be used in any position, as contrasted with *wu* 吾, which serves only as subject or possessive pronoun—'I', 'my'—or as the pre-verbal object in a negative sentence (cf. note 59).

63.   Here is an example of *ho* 何 in the adverbial position meaning 'how?'

64.   *ssu* 斯 occurs occasionally in the sense of 'then'. Its function is often similar to that of *tse* 則, i.e. to link the protasis and apodosis of a conditional sentence, but unlike *tse* 則 it can come after an imperative clause, as here. It is also used as a demonstrative adjective or pronoun (in Mencius only as an adjective)—'this', 'these'.

65.   *t'ien-hsia* 天下 is a compound noun formed from the noun *t'ien* 天 'heaven' and the postposition *hsia* 下 'under', cf. 'underground' in English. The 'under-heaven' means 'the world'. Notice that *hsia* 下 'below' and *shang* 上 'above' are not prepositions but postpositions in Chinese.

66.   *yen* 焉 'to him' is used here rather than 'to you' because the king is being referred to in the third person. The correct interpretation of pronouns in ancient Chinese is made more difficult by the fact that speakers commonly use the third person to refer both to themselves and to the person they are addressing.

PASSAGE C

PART of a conversation between Mencius and King Hsüan of Ch'i, an ancient and prosperous state in modern Shantung. King Hsüan reigned from 319 to 301 B.C. and was well known as a patron of learning. Huan of Ch'i and Wen of Chin, who are mentioned at the beginning of the conversation, date from the 7th Century B.C. They were the two most famous of the so-called *pa* or paramount princes who exercised hegemony over a group of Chinese states when the power of the Chou Dynasty declined, and they were therefore anathema to Confucius and Mencius, who lauded the sage founders of the Chou Dynasty (part of *Mencius* 1a. 7).

67.　　*k'o te wen hu* 可得聞乎 is a polite request for information—'may I be told about?' It is difficult to give a literal translation of this idiom. *k'o wen hu* 可聞乎 would mean 'may they be heard about?', so *k'o te wen hu* 可得聞乎 'may there be got a hearing about them?' The *hu* 乎 is irregular, *yü* 與 (which in this usage is a phonetic fusion of *yeh hu* 也乎, cf. note 87), appearing in all other occurrences of the idiom in Mencius. This is to be expected since in the indicative *k'o* 可 + passive verb is normally associated with the fin　particle *yeh* 也 (cf. note 55).

68.　　Chung-ni 仲尼 is the *tzu* 字 or 'style' of Confucius, the name by which it was polite to address him. His formal name was K'ung Ch'iu 孔丘, with the surname (姓 *hsing*), as always in Chinese, preceding the personal name (*ming* 名). The surname generally consists of one character, although there are a few surnames composed of two; but the personal name often consists of two characters.

69.　　For the *wu . . . che* 無 . . . 者 idiom cf. note 32, but notice that here we have a substantive preceding the *wu* 無 and going closely with it—'among the disciples of Confucius there were none who . . .', or alternatively, taking *wu* 無 as 'to lack', one can think of it as 'the disciples of Confucius lacked one who . . .'.

70.　　*shih i* 是以 'because of this' is a very common way of saying 'therefore'. As with the interrogative *ho i* 何以 the normal order of preposition preceding noun is reversed and the *i* 以 follows the pronoun. *i tz'u* 以此 also occurs, but as an adverbial phrase rather than as a conjunction.

71.　　The antecedent of *yen* 焉 is *hou shih* 後世—'therefore later generations have had nothing handed down *to them*'.

72.　　*ch'en* 臣 'minister', 'servant', is used frequently in appropriate cases instead of the first person pronoun—'your servant', 'I' (cf. the quasi-pronominal use of *kua-jen* 寡人 by kings referred to in note 28). The conventions of polite discourse meant that various humilific or honorific expressions came to function almost as first or second person pronouns.

73.　　The construction of *wei chih wen yeh* 未之聞也 is similar to that of *wei chih yu yeh* 未之有也 (cf. note 59), with the pronoun object *chih* 之 preceding the verb in the negative sentence, and with *yeh* 也, as often, associated with *wei* 未 (cf. note 25).

74.　　The subordinate clause here is causal: 'since I have no means (of discussing Huan and Wen), (shall I talk about) kingship?' The main clause lacks a verb, but this is easily supplied from the context.

Some would maintain that *wu i* 無以 is here just another way of writing the idiom *wu i* 無已 'if there is no getting out of it' (cf. *ju pu te i* 如不得已, see note 143), but *wu i* 無以 and its opposite *yu i* 有以 occur commonly and, as 'since I have no means' makes good sense here, there seems to be no compelling reason to adopt this other interpretation.

75.　　Literally this sentence reads 'If one's virtue resembles what, then can one become king?', i.e. 'with what sort of virtue may one become king?' Notice that *ho* 何 as object precedes the verb, just as it precedes the prepositional *i* 以 in *ho i* 何以. Notice also that the final particle *i* 矣 goes with *k'o i* 可以, whereas *k'o* 可 plus passive verb is associated with *yeh* 也 (cf. note 55).

76.　　Despite misleading definitions given in dictionaries *mo* 莫 always means 'nothing' or 'nobody'. It may stand independently as here, or be preceded by a noun limiting its range, e.g. *t'ien-hsia mo* 天下莫—'nobody in the world'. Notice that, after *mo* 莫 as after other negatives, the pronoun object *chih* 之 comes in the pre-verbal position. The sentence is appropriately terminated with *yeh* 也 because of the generality of the meaning of *mo* 莫 (cf. the use of *yeh* 也 with *wei* 未).

77.　　One should be quite clear about the difference between *k'o i* 可以 and *neng* 能, which occurs here for the first time. The latter means 'can' in the sense of 'have the ability to', and also occurs as a noun meaning 'ability'. *k'o i* 可以 means 'can' in the sense that the conditions—be they logical, physical, circumstantial, moral, or whatever—are such as to make it possible.

78.　　Like *ju* 如, *jo* 若 can mean both 'if' and 'to be like'. Here its function is obviously verbal because a verb is needed for the *che*-clause.

79.　　*tsai* 哉 is a particle which gives the sentence a flavour of exclamation or surprise: 'can someone like me *really* protect the people?' It is usually a final particle, but in certain idiomatic expressions it appears elsewhere in the sentence.

80.　　*ho yu* 何由, following the same pattern as *ho i* 何以, means 'from what?' On *yu* 由 see note 115.

81.　　*wu k'o yeh* 吾可也 is another example of indirect speech as explained in note 46. Here the *wu* 吾 ('my') is of course playing the part normally played by noun + possessive *chih* 之. Note that when the verb (in this case *pao* 保) is omitted after the auxiliary verb *k'o i* 可以, the *i* 以 drops off too.

82.　　Although the pronoun *chih* 之 is normally anaphoric, this is one common formula in which it refers forward—to an anecdote about to be related.

83.　　*shang* 上 here functions as a noun—'top of the hall'. *t'ang shang* 堂上 could also mean 'above the hall' with *shang* 上 functioning as a postposition. *shang* 上 cannot function as a preposition, so *shang t'ang* 上堂 would mean 'to mount the hall', with *shang* 上 functioning as a verb. The same rules apply to *hsia* 下 (cf. note 65).

84.　　Occasionally *chih* 之 means 'to go to', and here is an example which is fortunately not difficult to spot since without it the sentence would lack a verb. The construction of *ho chih* 何之 is the same as that of *ho ju* 何如 'what is it like?' (cf. note 42), so *ho chih* 何之 means 'what is it going to?', i.e. *'where* is it going?'

85. *i* 以 here means 'by means of *it*', 'with *it*'. It is used instead of *i chih* 以之, which never occurs.

86. *hu su* 觳觫 is an example of a type of rhyming two-character expression used to describe appearance, emotions, ritual attitudes, etc. Such expressions are used for their onomatopoeic effect, so the meanings of the characters used to write them are frequently irrelevant and they are used for their phonetic value only. *hu* 觳, for example, is normally the name of a vessel. Sometimes the expression may consist of one character repeated instead of two characters rhyming.

87. *yü* 與, as a final particle, is a phonetic fusion of *yeh hu* 也乎 and so is to be found in interrogative sentences when one would expect *yeh* 也 in the cognate indicative sentence.

88. *chu* 諸, as a final particle, is a phonetic fusion of *chih hu* 之乎. The parallelism between the *yu chu* 有諸 in the question and the *yu chih* 有之 ('it is so') in the reply demonstrates clearly that this is so. *chu* 諸 also occurs as a phonetic fusion of *chih yü* 之於 and as a collective prefix meaning 'all', 'the various' (cf. note 174).

   pu shih yu chu 不識有諸 means 'I do not know whether it happened'. Note that there is no function word like our 'whether' to serve to convert the direct into the indirect question. Taken literally, the Chinese says 'I do not know did-it-happen?'

89. *tsu* 足 means 'sufficient'. Just as *k'o i* 可以 goes with active verbs and *k'o* 可 with passive verbs, as explained in note 55, so *tsu i* 足以 goes with active verbs and *tsu* 足 with the passive. The former means 'capable of', 'adequate to', as here. For an example of the latter, see note 150.

90. *chieh* 皆 is a common word meaning 'all', usually, but not always, coming immediately after and referring to the subject of the sentence: 'The people *all* considered your majesty parsimonious'. The common idiom *i* 以 X *wei* 為 Y, 'to take X as being Y', 'to regard X as Y' should be noted.

91. See note 46.

92. *jan ch'eng yu pai hsing che* 然誠有百姓者 is a puzzling clause which has been variously interpreted. Perhaps the safest translation is 'Yes, there really are such people', but this does not make very satisfactory sense of the *che* 者.

93. *sui* 雖 means 'although', 'even if' and in the great majority of cases, but not always, it follows the subject of the concessive clause, as it does here. Sometimes it goes with a noun rather than a clause, and means 'even a'. Thus *sui hsiao kuo* 雖小國 would mean 'even a small state'.

94. *chi* 即 probably means 'it so happened that', 'actually', 'at that moment', but since it only occurs once as a grammatical word in Mencius it is not easy to

be certain. Its most common function in texts of the period is as an alternative to *tse* 則.

95.　*ku* 故 is a common word for 'therefore', 'consequently', or 'and that is why'. As a general rule, when the *ku* 故 links two clauses in narrative sequence ('therefore', 'consequently'), the *ku*-clause does not terminate with *yeh* 也, but when the *ku*-clause gives an explanation ('and that is why'), it naturally terminates with *yeh* 也. In this context the replacing of an ox by a sheep has already been narrated, and here the king is giving an explanation of his conduct. Cf. the distinction between *shih i* 是以 and *shih i . . . yeh* 是以 . . . 也 described in note 106.

96.　*pi* 彼 is a demonstrative pronoun or adjective, meaning 'that', 'those', in contrast with *tz'u* 此, meaning 'this', 'these'. Here, as often, it means 'those people', 'they'. Unlike *tz'u* 此, which often refers to circumstances, conditions, situations, *pi* 彼 is a much less common word and generally, but not always, has a concrete reference, e.g. 'that man'.

97.　*wu* 惡 is here an interrogative. It appears in the adverbial position and means 'how' in this context.

98.　*jo* 若 here appears to mean 'if', but with the *tse* 則 linking subordinate clause to main clause no word for 'if' is really necessary. Furthermore, in earlier parallels to this sentence there is a *jo* 若 before the *wu tsui* 無罪, and it therefore seems possible that the *jo* 若 here is misplaced and should really go before the *wu tsui* 無罪 in this sentence too. Arguments from parallelism like this are often used when textual emendations are proposed.

99.　The *yen* 焉 refers back to the *niu yang* 牛羊—'an ox and a sheep—how choose between them?' i.e. 'how does one choose between an ox and a sheep?' or, as we would say idiomatically, 'what is there to choose between an ox and a sheep?'

100.　Notice the construction of this sentence. *ho* 何 here functions as an interrogative adjective and occupies exactly the same position in the sentence as would be filled by an adjective supplied to answer the question. The sentence translated word for word in the Chinese order reads 'this is really what mind?' but in English we have to say something like 'what really were my motives in this?'

101.　*fei* 非 here negates the whole sentence—'it is not the case that', 'it is not true that' (cf. note 61). Since the function of the sentence is to reject an explanation, it naturally concludes with *yeh* 也.

102.　Apart from its uses as a final interrogative particle, *hu* 乎 sometimes occurs as an alternative for the preposition *yü* 於. This is its usual function when it is not final, and it has been interpreted in this sense here by some scholars ('there was reason in . . .'). But occasionally it occurs in a non-final position as an interjection with interrogative or exclamatory force, and it is probably best to take it in that sense—'was it reasonable that . . .?' or 'it was reasonable indeed that . . .'.

103.　　*nai* 乃 is a grammatical word which is not very common, but apparently has several different functions, so it is not easy to translate. Occupying this position in the non-verbal sentence it seems to mean 'in fact', 'really'. Thus X *nai* 乃 Y *yeh* 也 means 'X really is Y'.

104.　　This is another example of *yeh* 也 exposing certain elements of a sentence and making them into a kind of heading or psychological subject. Note 28 discusses a similar example, but there the *yü*-phrase is resumed by a *yen* 焉 whereas here the *ch'i* 其 refers back to the noun dependent on the *yü* 於.

105　　Notice the idiom here. The Chinese says 'see their life' and 'see their death' whereas we should say 'see them living' and 'see them dead'.

106.　　Notice the difference between this *shih i* 是以 and the one near the beginning of the passage (see note 70). Here we are given an explanation for a general principle of conduct ('and that is why gentlemen keep their kitchens at a distance'), so the clause is concluded with *yeh* 也. In the other example the *shih i* 是以 records a consequence in narrative sequence—'A didn't happen and *therefore* B didn't happen'. Cf. the distinction between *ku* 故 and *ku* . . . *yeh* 故 . . . 也 pointed out in note 95.

PASSAGE D

DUKE P'ing of Lu, the state which was famous as the birthplace of Confucius, does not call on Mencius because of Mencius's alleged lack of propriety. Yo-cheng Tzu, a former pupil of Mencius now employed at the Lu court, argues in Mencius's favour (*Mencius*, 1b. 16).

107.　　The use of *che* 者 after the name of a person is an idiom which in the opinion of some authorities has the force of our 'a certain . . .', i.e. 'a certain Tsang Ts'ang', but which in later usage makes little or no addition to the sense. For example, in biographies in the famous Han Dynasty historical work known as the *Shih chi* it appears after the name of the subjects of the biographies when they first occur, as if to underline them.

108.　　Observe that *yu-ssu* 有司 is a verb-object compound noun meaning 'office-holder', 'official'. It is formed in the same way as such English nouns as 'spoil-sport'.

109.　　Although it is a very important and quite common function word, we meet *so* 所 here for the first time. It is generally a relative pronoun translatable as 'what', 'those whom', 'that which', etc., i.e. substituting for the object of a cognate simple verbal sentence. Thus compare *ming yu-ssu* 命有司 'I instruct my officers' with *chien so ming* 見所命 'I visit *those whom* I instruct'; and compare *chien niu* 見牛 'I saw the ox' with *so chien niu yeh* 所見牛也 'what I saw was the ox'. But since what follows the verb may not be a direct object, but an expression denoting distance, destination, etc., *so* 所 may be translatable in English by such relative adverbial expressions as 'how far', 'where', etc., Compare, for example, *chih Lu* 之魯 'I am going to Lu' with *chih so chih* 知所之 'I know where I am going'. Similarly the interrogative *ho* 何 is translatable as 'where?' in such sentences as *ho chih* 何之 'where is it going?', as we observed in note 84.

Apart from its grammatical uses *so* 所 also occurs as a noun meaning 'place'.

110.   In the sense of 'now' *chin* 今 does not, like most adverbs, go closely with the verb, but nearly always occurs at the beginning, setting the time for the whole sentence. Sometimes it introduces a conditional clause—'if now', 'if', and sometimes it functions as an adjective or noun, meaning 'the present'.

111.   Like *chi* 既 (see note 38) *i* 已 functions as a temporal auxiliary indicating that the action of the verb is completed—'The horses have already been harnessed to the carriage'. The basic meaning of the character is 'to finish' (cf. the idiom *erh i* 而已) and the usage we are here describing arises naturally from that.

112.   *so* 所 also occurs in combination with various prepositions: e.g. *so tz'u* 所自 ('that from which', 'whence'), *so yü* 所與 ('the one with whom'), *so wei* 所為 ('the one on behalf of whom', 'that because of which', 'the reason why'), and—much the most common—*so i* 所以 ('that by means of which', 'the means whereby', 'the reason why').

Notice that the subject of the *so*-clause precedes the *so* 所. Often it is linked with the *so*-clause by means of a possessive *chih* 之, which is due to the fact that the *so*-clause is always a noun-clause and is to be regarded as interchangeable with a noun: thus, compare *hsien wang chih tao* 先王之道 'the way of the ancient kings' with *hsien wang chih so hsing* 先王之所行 'the what-practised of the ancient kings', i.e. 'what the ancient kings practised'.

Notice also that the *so*-clause is terminated by a *che* 者. This adds nothing to the sense but merely serves to mark off the end of the clause. Without some such device it might not always be clear where a *so*-clause terminated.

The prepositional usage of *wei* 為—'for', 'on behalf of', 'because of'—should also be noted.

113.   The *i* 以 here introduces a consequence clause—'so as to'.

114.   *i wei hsien* 以為賢 means 'regard *him* as a man of virtue'. As has already been pointed out in note 85, *i chih* 以之 never occurs, so this is simply a special case of the *i* . . . *wei* 以 . . . 為 idiom (cf. note 90).

In this sentence *so wei* 所為 and *i wei hsien* 以為賢 must be taken in conjunction with each other. The idiom *so wei* (or *so i*) . . ., *i* . . . 所為 (所以) . . ., 以 . . . means 'the reason why . . . is because . . .'. Although two *is* seem to be needed, one for this idiom and one for the *i wei* 以為 idiom, one of them drops out.

115.   *yu* 由 is a preposition meaning 'from'. It is a directional 'from' (like the 'from' in 'from London to Peking') and is therefore generally associated with verbs of motion such as *ch'u* 出, *lai* 來, *hsing* 行, *chih* 至. The pattern is *yu* 由 -noun-verb. By contrast *yü* 於 meaning 'from' always comes after the verb and is the 'from' in 'take away from'.

For *hsien che* 賢者 cf. note 54.

41

116.　　Just as in English we can say either 'visit' or 'pay a visit *to*', 'call *on*', so in Chinese we sometimes find *yen* 焉 rather than *chih* 之 after the verb *chien* 見. Sometimes, however, the presence of a *yü* 於 after a verb may make a great difference to its meaning. In the previous line, for example, *hsien yü* 先於 means 'pay the first visit *to*', but *hsien* 先 by itself would mean 'give preference to', 'put first' (cf. note 21).

117.　　The interrogative *hsi* 奚 operates in much the same way as *ho* 何, and *hsi wei* 奚為 means the same as *ho wei* 何為—'for what reason?'
　　But unlike *ho* 何, *hsi* 奚 never functions as an adjective.

118.　　The verb in a *so*-clause is not normally followed by an object, because the *so* 所 itself is the object of the verb. Here we have an exception to the rule, the case of the verb *wei* 謂 'to call', which takes two objects: '*what* you call "*exceeding*"'.

119.　　It looks as if the two *i*'s 以 here are being used as main verbs, but I think it is better to regard them as prepositions with the expected verb eventually omitted because it is easily understood from the context; i.e., 'on the earlier occasion (practised mourning) with three cauldrons, and on the later with five'. The same, of course, applies to the *i shih* 以士 and *i tai-fu* 以大夫 earlier in the sentence; but there the language is even more economical, so that the former must be translated 'in accordance with (the ritual appropriate to) a knight' or 'as a knight', and *i tai-fu* 一大夫 must be treated in the same way.

120.　　The *yü* 與 (which is a fusion of *yeh hu* 也乎) comes appropriately here because the question is not whether a certain event occurred, but whether a certain explanation is true.

121.　　*fou* 否 often stands as a single-word answer to a question, as here. It means 'No' or 'I do not', here standing for 'No, I do not mean that'. In other words it substitutes for a negative verbal sentence (a sentence negated by *pu* 不) made in reply to a formal question. It might be termed 'the proclausal negative'. Similarly in indirect questions it means 'or not', substituting for the negative version of the clause just given in the positive (cf. note 141).

122.　　*fei* 非 here negatives a non-verbal sentence in which the subject is not expressed.

123.　　A case of the privative *pu* 不, *pu-t'ung* 不同 meaning 'dissimilarity'.

124.　　*K'e* 克 is the speaker's own name. Personal names are often used like this instead of the first person pronoun.

125.　　This is a very unusual sense of *wei* 為 related, I think, to the common meaning 'on behalf of', but here verbal—'the king was in favour of coming to see you'. It is reminiscent of the English colloquialism 'to be "pro" doing something or other'.

126.　　Note that this time, as compared with the passage discussed in note 107, there is a *yu* 有 between the *pi jen* 嬖人 and the *Tsang Ts'ang* 臧倉 so the translation is: 'among his favourites there is a certain Tsang Ts'ang' or 'one of his favourites, a certain Tsang Ts'ang'. In such contexts as this *yu* 有 provides an equivalent of the pronouns 'one' and 'some'.

127.   The grammatical use of *kuo* 果 is easily understood when the non-grammatical meaning of the word—'fruit'—is borne in mind. It is used when a proposed course of action is described as coming to fruition. Thus *kuo lại* 果來 would mean that, the king having proposed to come, 'he did *actually* come'. Here 'he did not *actually* come'.

128.   This sentence means: 'If a man makes progress, something is sending him on his way, and if a man stops, something is hindering him.' Notice that the use of *huo . . . huo . . .* 或 . . . 或 . . . is different from that explained in note 39, where it meant 'some . . . others . . .'. In that example the *huos* referred to two different groups of people, but here the 'something' may be the same thing in each instance.

129.   Although *so* 所 normally functions as a relative pronoun, the verbal sentence of which this *so*-clause is a permutation is *jen neng hsing, hih* 人能行止 'others are able to advance or stop him'. So here the *so* 所 is in fact substituting for the *verbs* which follow the auxiliary verb *neng* 能. The reason why this can happen is that *hsing* 行 and *chih* 止 'advancing' and 'stopping' have already occurred as nouns at the beginning of the sentence, so it is as if the *hsing* 行 and *chih* 止 substituted for by *so* 所 are the *objects* of *neng* 能. The sentence we have means 'advancing or stopping (him) is not what other men are capable of'.

130.   The *chih* 之 here performs the common function of neatly forming a substantival clause—'my not meeting' or 'the fact that I did not meet', but it is rather surprising to find it here since *wu* 吾 is already possessive. *wu chih* 吾之 does, however, occur elsewhere in Mencius.

131.   *yen* 焉, which we have met several times as a final particle, also occurs as an interrogative adverb meaning 'how?', 'in what respect?', 'where?' Just as the final particle *yen* 焉 stands for *yü* + *chih* 於之, so the interrogative *yen* 焉 seems to be equivalent to *yü* 於 + interrogative pronoun ('in what respect', 'to/in what place'). In combination with the exclamatory final particle *tsai* 哉, as here, it forms a rhetorical question.

132.   *yü* 予 is a first person pronoun which is archaic and relatively uncommon in Mencius as compared with *wu* 吾 and *wo* 我. It occurs as either subject or object, but unlike *wu* 吾 and *wo* 我 it is never found as a possessive pronoun in Mencius.

PASSAGE E

MENCIUS is reproached for not calling on King Hsuan of Ch'i, but he argues that no-one else in Ch'i shows such respect for the king as he does. Of the people mentioned, Kung-sun Ch'ou was a disciple of Mencius, Meng Chung-tzu is said to have been his nephew, and nothing is known about the Tung-kuo family and Ching Ch'ou (*Mencius*, IIb. 2).

133.   I do not find any of the interpretations of this *ju* 如 in translations and commentaries at all satisfactory. It has been taken to mean either 'ought to' or 'intended to' or 'desired to' but none of these meanings is found elsewhere in Mencius, nor do they account satisfactorily for the *che* 者. On the other hand it seems to me that satisfactory sense may be obtained by taking *ju* 如 in the normal sense of 'to be like', i.e. 'I was like one who was going to see you', in other words 'I was as good as going to see you'.

134.   *feng* 風 here has the unusual verbal sense of 'to face the wind', 'to endure the wind'.

135.   This sentence consists of a polite circumlocution: literally 'I do not know whether it may be brought about that I am able to see you'. *te* 得, which in its non-grammatical sense means 'to get', 'to obtain', has a closely related grammatical usage as an auxiliary verb with the sense of 'to *get to* do', 'to *succeed in* doing', 'to *manage to* do'. Often the most natural translation is 'to be able', which is how I have rendered it in this context, but it must be remembered that it never means 'to be able' in the sense of 'to have the ability to', for this idea is rendered by *neng* 能. There is a much clearer distinction in Classical Chinese than in English between words of this and related meanings. In this connection it is interesting to notice what a difference tense may make to the meaning of an English verb: 'I am able to' means 'I have the ability to' (*neng* 能); but 'I was able to' means 'I succeeded in' (*te* 得).

     Notice that we have here another indirect question (cf. note 88).

136.   *hsi che* 昔者 'formerly' is a common temporal expression nearly always occurring at the beginning of the sentence and establishing the time of the passage. This introduces us to a new function of *che* 者, for there are various other words which may be set off by *che* 者 in this way, e.g. *chin che* 今者 'now', *ku che* 古者 'in antiquity', and *huo che* 或者 'perhaps' (which occurs later in this same column of text). Notice the term *chin jih* 今日, meaning 'today', which balances the *hsi che* 昔者.

137.   Note that *pu k'o* 不可 here, as often, carries the definite sense of impropriety—'perhaps this should not have been done', 'perhaps this was improper' (cf. note 55).

138.   *ju chih ho* 如之何 is a common expression meaning 'it being like this, why?', 'in such circumstances, why . . .?'.

139.   Note the pronominal use of *jen* 人—'someone'.

140.   'The sorrow of gathering firewood' is taken as a polite way of referring to illness, but the reason for the expression is not clear. It may mean 'I am confined to my quarters (and therefore have the trouble of gathering fuel to light a fire), or I am too unwell even to gather firewood'.

141.   Here we have an indirect question of the 'whether or not' type, with the proclausal *fou* 否 standing for 'or not'. On *fou* 否 see note 121.

142.   The combination of *ch'ing* 請 and *pi* 必 involves a usage of *pi* 必 which is slightly different from the normal. 'I beg you to make a point of not returning' or 'I beg you to be sure not to return' is the meaning of the sentence.

143.   *pu te i* 不得已 (literally, 'cannot finish', 'cannot get rid of') and *ju pu te i* 如不得已 (literally, 'if cannot finish', 'if cannot get rid of') are idioms meaning 'not being able to avoid it', 'having no alternative'.

144.   This kind of pattern, with *tse* 則 being preceded by a single word rather than by a clause, will be encountered quite frequently. The meaning of *tse* 則 remains basically the same, but the idiom has to be rendered by a rather different turn of phrase in English. The crude literal translation would be: 'If inside then the father-son (relationship), if outside then the ruler-minister (relationship), are the important relationships of men.' The effect is to place some emphasis on the *nei* 內 and the *wai* 外, and the idiom may perhaps best be rendered here by 'in the home on the one hand . . . outside the family on the other hand . . .'. This translation is obviously not open to us when we meet this idiom with a single *tse* 則 rather than with a *tse* 則 in two parallel sentences, as here; and in such cases some such circumlocution as 'if we are talking about X' or 'as far as X is concerned' or 'as for X' is often necessary.

145.   Notice how the *fu tzu* 父子 is, as it were, hyphenated by the context and the sentence-pattern to mean the 'father-son (relationship)'.

146.   A clause like *wang chih ching tzu yeh* 王之敬子也 can obviously be rendered either 'that the king respects you, Master' or 'the king's respect for you, Master'. The language makes no difference between the two. Mencius is, as often, referred to as *tzu* 子 rather than addressed with the second person pronoun, the usage being so common that it may virtually be regarded as pronominal (cf. note 72).

147.   *wu* 惡, which we have already met as an interrogative, is here an interjection—'oh!' The whole sentence forms an exclamation meaning 'Oh! these are what words!', i.e. 'Oh! what a thing to say!' (cf. note 100 for an explanation of the word-order in a similar sentence).

148.   In this *wu . . . che* 無 . . . 者 construction the verb does not come till immediately before the *che* 者. The use of *i* 以 in the sense of 'about' is regular with the verb *kao* 告 meaning 'to tell', and it is here used with the verb *yen* 言 in the same sense; but *yen* 言 more commonly means 'to talk *about*' and is followed directly by the topic of conversation. Thus 'to talk about benevolence and justice' would normally be *yen jen i* 言仁義, which does in fact occur in the next column.

149.   The function of *ch'i* 豈 is to form a rhetorical question. It may be translated 'how?' or 'surely not?' In a verbal sentence it naturally appears in the adverbial position, and in a non-verbal sentence it occupies a position like that of *fei* 非 between subject and predicate. In the great majority of cases the exclamatory final particle *tsai* 哉 forms a natural conclusion to a sentence containing

ch'i 豈. The reason why this sentence is terminated with *yeh* 也 is that the clause is explanatory rather than narrative, i.e. it is not 'surely they do not regard humanity and justice as undesirable', but rather 'surely it is not that (or, not because) they regard humanity and justice as undesirable'. In other words, although it looks like a verbal sentence, the *yeh* 也 gives it the flavour of the X Y *yeh* construction, which, if Y is a clause, often constitutes an explanation ('X is the fact that Y', and so 'X implies Y' or 'X is because Y'); as, for example, in Mencius 1a.7, where *wang chih pu wang pu wei yeh, fei pu neng yeh* 王之不王不爲也，非不能也 means 'Your Majesty's not being a true king is *because* you do not, not *because* you cannot'. Compare also the sentence-pattern 'X *ho yeh*' X 何也, discussed in note 34.

150.   This is a case of *tsu* 足 being followed by a passive verb (cf. note 89), but here room has to be found for the preposition *yü* 與 which goes closely with the verb. The sentence means 'how is this person fit to be talked humanity and justice with?' Chinese can do this very neatly but it is very clumsy in English, and we had better say something like 'this man is not fit to be conversed with about humanity and justice'.

We have now met *yü* 與 in three different senses: (1) as a preposition—'together with'; (2) as a coordinate conjunction—'and'; and (3) as a phonetic fusion of *yeh hu* 也乎. It also has two common verbal meanings—'to present' and 'to associate with', and it occurs as an adverb ('together', 'jointly'), an adjective ('friendly', 'allied'), and a noun ('alliance', 'party', 'share'). The earliest form of the graph shows one pair of hands giving an object to, or sharing an object with, another pair of hands, so it will be seen that all the meanings of the word stem naturally from this (excluding, of course, its usage to write the phonetic fusion of *yeh hu* 也乎).

151.   *yün erh* 云爾 is a rather rare combination of grammatical words. The word *yün* 云 is normally used to introduce a quotation: thus *Shih yün* 詩云 means 'The Book of Songs says'. But sometimes, as here, it serves to mark off the end of a quotation. The *erh* 爾 (which can also mean 'you') is here another way of writing the phonetic fusion of *erh i* 而已 (we have already met 耳 used for this purpose, see note 29). So the whole sentence may be translated: 'If they simply (*erh* 爾) think (lit. 'say in their hearts'): "This fellow is not worth conversing with about humanity and justice", then that is the greatest possible disrespect'.

152.   The idiom *mo ta hu* (or *yü*) 莫大乎 (於) 'nothing greater than' is very common. In English it is often more natural to use a superlative, as I have done in the translation given above in note 151. Notice the privative use of *pu* 不 in *pu ching* 不敬 'disrespect'. This is, of course, not really a difference in function of the *pu* 不, but simply the effect of the nominalization of *ching* 敬 (cf. note 20). Notice also the behaviour of *mo* 莫: instead of the negative word preceding the noun as in 'no disrespect' in English, *mo* 莫 'none', 'nothing' is preceded by and therefore qualified by the *pu ching* 不敬 'disrespect'—'nothing of disrespect'.

For the use of *hu* 乎 for *yü* 於, cf. note 102.

153.　　Notice this idiom with *fei* 非 and *pu* 不: 'if not the way of Yao and Shun, I do not venture to set it before the king'. This provides the equivalent of 'anything but' in English, i.e. 'I do not venture to set before the king *anything but* the way of Yao and Shun'.

154.　　Notice that *ch'en* 陳 does not take the direct object *chih* 之. Instead, the thing given is introduced by the preposition *i* 以 (cf. English 'to present someone *with* something'). So here *i* 以 stands for *i chih* 以之 and literally means 'with it', referring back to the *Yao Shun chih tao* 堯舜之道. Other verbs meaning 'to give', e.g. *yü* 與, also operate with *i* 以 in the same way.

155.　　The pattern exemplified in *yü wang ch'ien* 於王前, 'in front of the king', should be noted. It also occurs in such phrases as *yü* X *shang* 於 X 上 and *yü* X *hsia* 於 X 下, 'above X' and 'below X'.

156.　　Compare this use of *mo* 莫 with the one discussed in note 152. Here *mo* 莫 qualified by *Ch'i jen* 齊人—'none of the men of Ch'i'—conforms completely with the English idiom and so is much more readily understandable than *pu ching mo* 不敬莫 'nothing of disrespect'.

157.　　Here we have the use of *ju* 如 in an idiom which is the equivalent of our 'as much as'. *ju wo ching wang* 如我敬王 means 'respects the king as much as I do'. We say 'as much as I', but the Chinese says 'like me', 'doing like me', retaining the verbal quality of *ju* 如 with *wo* 我 as object.

GRAMMATICAL SURVEY

In these five passages from Mencius, amounting to little more than one thousand characters in all, we find that a very high proportion of the constructions and of the words of grammatical interest met with in late Chou Chinese literature are found, so that once the grammar of these passages is thoroughly understood, the student should be able to proceed with confidence to the remaining passages, knowing that he has only to fill in gaps which are more a problem of vocabulary than of understanding radically new constructions. I therefore propose to survey the grammatical knowledge so far acquired before I discuss the further passages.

It will already be obvious that there are certain function words which occur very frequently and play key parts in the structure of the language. The most common characters in the passages we have read so far are *chih* 之, *yeh* 也, *pu* 不, *i* 以, *che* 者, and *erh* 而, every fifth character being on average one of these six. Add to them *so* 所, *yü* 於, and *tse* 則, and we have a list of the most important function words in the language. Most of them occur so frequently that we have already collected sufficient material to enable us to understand them, while at the same time they are the most important function words for us to understand. Thus we have two good reasons for dealing with this group of key function words first, and I shall accordingly proceed to do so, omitting only *pu* 不, which is better reserved for discussion with the other negatives, and *tse* 則, which is dealt with more conveniently in section F.

A. The Key Function Words

1. *chih* 之

We have seen that the most common use of *chih* 之 is as a possessive or determinative particle. The latter usage we met early on in the expression *wan ch'eng chih kuo* 萬乘之國, in which the concept 'state' is determined or limited to 'state of ten thousand chariots' (see note 15). The possessive usage is closely related to this, e.g. *lin kuo chih min* 鄰國之民 'the people of neighbouring states'. In these two examples there is no formal distinction between the possessive and the determinative. In more complicated constructions, however, there is a clear formal distinction between the two usages. In the possessive pattern there is only one substantive before the *chih* 之, even in the most complicated constructions, e.g. *min chih to yü lin kuo* 民之多於鄰國 'the people's becoming more numerous than neighbouring states'; but in the determinative pattern the single substantive comes last, as in *ch'i yü pu hsiang ai chih luan* 起於不相愛之亂 'disorder that arises from not loving each other'.

The use of *chih* 之 to form a substantival clause is a neat and useful device, of especial importance being its occurrence in indirect speech after verbs of saying, knowing, etc., as in *wang min chih to yü lin kuo yeh* 望民之多於鄰國也

48

'expect that the people will become more numerous than neighbouring states' (see note 46).

The other common grammatical usage of *chih* 之 is as a third person pronoun which normally comes immediately after the verb and supplies its object ('him', 'her', 'it', 'them'). It is usually anaphoric, but not necessarily so, for sometimes no antecedent is mentioned, and note 82 gives an example of a common formula in which *chih* 之 is not anaphoric. Points we have noticed about the behaviour of the pronoun *chih* 之 are (1) that it precedes the verb in negative constructions, e.g. *mo chih neng yü yeh* 莫之能禦也 (see note 76); and (2) that it is sometimes replaced by fusion forms, such as *chu* 諸, standing for *chih hu* 之乎 or *chih yü* 之於 (see note 88), *yen* 焉, standing for *yü chih* 於之 (see note 19), and probably *wu* 勿, standing for *wu chih* 毋之 (see note 57).

2. *yeh* 也

yeh 也 is of all function words found in this literature only less common than *chih* 之, but scholars have found difficulty in giving a thoroughly satisfactory account of it. We have, however, already been able to make certain observations about its use, and in all cases *yeh* 也 seems to have the quality of affirming or emphasizing what precedes.

(1) It occurs after the predicate (the 'Y' element) in a non-verbal (XY 也 = 'X is Y') kind of sentence (see note 34). Here it would be reasonable to believe that its function is partly to lay stress on the newly given term, i.e. 'X is Y'.

(2) It marks off certain elements at the beginning of a sentence again apparently for emphasis, as in the example *kua-jen chih yü kuo yeh* 寡人之於國也 (see note 28).

(3) It is commonly part of the construction with *chih* 之 to record indirect speech (see note 46). These clauses intrinsically possess the quality of affirmation which we have associated with *yeh* 也.

(4) The most difficult usage of *yeh* 也 to explain satisfactorily is when it comes as a final particle in a verbal sentence. Here perhaps the best way of thinking of it is that it partakes of the quality of the non-verbal ('X is Y') type of sentence, the essence of which is that it does not record acts, but judgements, does not describe momentary events but continuing states. Thus we noticed that *wei* 未 'never' is accompanied by *yeh* 也, never by *i* 矣, the final particle which, by contrast with *yeh* 也, gives a quality of completeness or of happening once and for all to the verb of the clause it terminates (see note 25).

If we look for contrasts between *yeh* 也 and *i* 矣 in the material we have read so far (omitting usages of *yeh* 也 explicable under 1-3 above) the distinction will become clearer. In Passage A we notice two examples of *yeh* 也 associated with *wei* 未 (6a and 6j). By contrast there is the *kuo wei i* 國危矣 (3t) 'the state will be endangered, brought into danger' (implying a once-and-for-all occurrence). Notice also that *i* 矣 is to be found with an imperative (6r): commands, expecting once-and-for-all obedience, are naturally terminated with *i* 矣 rather than with *yeh* 也.

In Passage B there is a contrast between several instances of *yeh* 也 terminating sentences with *k'o* 可 + passive verb and *i* 矣 terminating sentences with *k'o i* 可以 + active verb. The force of the *i* 矣 might be suggested by translating 15 m–t as 'it will *become* possible for fifty-year-olds to wear silk'.

In Passage C the *i* 矣 after the *k'o i wang* 可以王 and *tsu i wang* 足以王 is satisfactorily rendered by translating *wang* 王 as 'become king', rather than 'be king'. *ku i yang i chih yeh* 故以羊易之也 (29 g–l) does not narrate an incident but gives an explanation or judgement—'that was the reason why I changed it for sheep'. This may be compared with the *fei*-clause terminated with *yeh* 也 rejecting an explanation—'it is not the case that I changed it for a sheep because I begrudged the expense of it' (31 f–p). In *wei chien yang yeh* 未見羊也 we come to another example of a *wei . . . yeh* construction. Finally in the *shih i . . . yeh* 是以 . . . 也 (that is why . . .') (33 l–s), there is another explanatory or judgemental sentence.

In Passage D we find *i* 矣 coming naturally after the temporal auxiliary *i* 已 (35 c) and *yeh* 也 coming after a *hsi wei* 奚為 (37 m–n) and a *shih i* 是以 (38 h–i), asking and giving explanations. In *chün wei lai chien yeh* 君為來見也 we have a description of the *chün's* state or condition—'he was disposed to come and see you' (40 s–w).

In Passage E the *ch'i i jen i wei pu mei yeh* 豈以仁義為不美也 (50 x–51 e) again gives an explanation—'surely it was not because . . .'; and the last sentence, beginning with *ku* 故, gives an explanation and is therefore naturally concluded with *yeh* 也 (52 u).

3. *i* 以

The common use of the word *i* 以 is, as we have seen, as a preposition in the sense of 'by means of'. A variety of other translations have to be used according to context, but all derive naturally from the basic meaning 'to use'. Thus *i shih* 以時 'using the seasons' means 'according to the season' or 'in season'.

We have noticed the common expressions *ho i* 何以 'by means of what?', 'how?', and *shih i* 是以 'by means of this', 'because of this', 'therefore', in which the *i* 以 is postpositional.

We have also noticed that occasionally the *i*-phrase comes after the verb instead of in its natural position preceding, and so qualifying, the verb. This sometimes occurs for reasons of emphasis, as in *shu chih i sang* 樹之以桑 (see note 53) and sometimes merely for the sake of the balance of the sentence.

There are various idiomatic ways in which *i* 以 + noun is used, e.g. with verbs of giving the preposition *i* 以 introduces the thing given, like 'to present *with*' in English (cf. note 154). A similar construction occurs with *kao* 告 and *yen* 言 'to tell', where the thing told is introduced by *i* 以 (cf. note 148).

Another point to remember is that *i chih* 以之 never occurs, so that *i* 以 by itself often means 'with it' or 'thereby' (see note 85).

i 以 introducing a clause is much less common than the prepositional *i* 以. An *i*-clause following the main clause and lacking a subject is a purpose or consequence clause ('in order to' or 'so as to'), but with a subject it expresses cause or reason.

We took note of the idiom *i wei* 以為 or *i . . . wei . . .* 以 . . . 為 'to regard as' (see note 90), and the occurrence of *i* 以 in *k'o i* 可以 and *tsu i* 足以 (see notes 55 and 89).

4. *che* 者

We have become aware that the most common use of *che* 者 is to convert a verbal sentence into a substantival clause with the sense of 'he who . . .', 'those who . . .', etc. Thus *ai jen che* 愛人者 may mean 'those who love others'. Another meaning is, however, possible: 'love of others' (cf. note 59). This is simply an extension of the fact that any verb-object combination in Chinese can either constitute a verbal clause or a verb-object substantive, i.e. *shih chun* 弒君 could mean either 'he assassinated the ruler' or 'assassination', and *ai jen* 愛人, which would normally mean 'he loves others' could mean 'love of others' in, for example, *chiao ai-jen* 教愛人 'he teaches love of others'. Just as the former is by far the most common way of taking *ai jen* 愛人, so *ai jen che* 愛人者 would in the great majority of cases be 'he who, those who, love others'. But one should always be on the alert for the other possibility. Thus, *sha ch'i mi-lu che ju sha jen chih tsui* 殺其麋鹿者如殺人之罪 in *Mencius* 1b.2 must be translated 'killing its deer is equal to the crime of killing men'. The sentence will not work out properly if one translates: 'those who kill its deer'.

We have also encountered the following minor uses of *che* 者:

i. By extension of its use after a clause, it sometimes occurs with a non-verbal word or phrase with similar effect, i.e. to indicate a class of people, e.g. *wu shih che* 五十者 'those who are fifty', 'fifty-year-olds' (see note 54).

ii. After names of persons, meaning 'a certain . . .'? (see note 107).

iii. To mark the end of a *so* 所-clause (see note 112).

iv. In the expressions *hsi che* 昔者 'formerly' and *huo che* 或者 'perhaps' (see note 136).

There are two more minor usages which have not yet been encountered: (a) with numbers, e.g. *san che* 三者 means 'these three things'; (b) in giving definitions, e.g. *ming t'ang che wang che chih t'ang yeh* 明堂者王者之堂也 (in *Mencius* 1b.5) means 'the word "ming-t'ang" means the hall of one who rules as a king' (the second *che* 者 is, of course, an example of the most common function of *che* 者, *wang* 王 there being verbal).

5. *erh* 而

The conjunction *erh* 而 has been a very controversial word in Chinese grammatical studies. Attempts to reach too precise a definition of its meaning rather than its function are misguided, because its importance lies in the part it plays in the structure of sentences. What is clear about *erh* 而 is that it usually separates two clauses and that, for translation purposes, it works best not simply to render it as 'and' or 'but' but to take it as subordinating the clause which precedes it to the clause which follows it. But we should not apply this rule too dogmatically since there are cases where we find that we have to regard the clause preceding the *erh* 而 as the main clause and the clause succeeding the *erh* 而 as a purpose or consequence clause. There are also difficulties which arise from the fact that the *erh* 而 is sometimes preceded, not by a clause, but by a word or phrase, but we will not discuss this type of construction since we have not met any examples.

6. *so* 所

Generally speaking *so* 所 functions as a relative pronoun serving as the object of its clause, and translatable as 'what', 'that which', 'those whom', etc. Thus *chien niu* 見牛 means 'he sees an ox' and *chih Lu* 之魯 means 'he goes to Lu'; and if the objects of these two sentences are replaced with *so* 所, we have *so chien* 所見 meaning 'what he sees', and *so chih* 所之, 'what he is going to', i.e. '*where* he is going'. In the latter example the sense of *so* 所 is very reminiscent of the word's non-grammatical meaning, which is 'place'. Thus *chih so chih* 知所之 'I know where I am going' might equally well be translated 'I know the place I am going to'.

The *so*-clause, as we have noticed, becomes syntactically interchangeable with a noun, for what appears in translation as the subject of the clause comes outside the clause and is often linked to it with a possessive *chih* 之 just as if the *so*-clause were an ordinary noun. For example compare *hsien wang chih tao* 先王之道 'the way of the ancient kings' with *hsien wang chih so hsing* 先王之所行, 'the what-practised of the ancient kings', i.e. 'what the ancient kings practised'.

Normally, since the *so* 所 itself supplies the object of the *so*-clause there is no object following the verb, but we have noted one situation in which an object does occur, viz. with a verb which takes two objects, like *wei* 謂 'to call' (see note 118). Another situation in which one meets *so*-verb-object, is when the *so* 所 means 'that for which' and substitutes for the purpose clause which would normally follow the object in the sentence of which the *so*-clause is a permutation. Thus compare *so yung chih i yeh* 所用之異也 'the purpose for which they used it was different' with *yung chih* 用之 followed by a verb—'they used it *to do so-and-so*'. The *so* 所 in the former clearly corresponds with the *to do so-and-so* in the latter (see also note 251).

We have also noticed that *so* 所 is used with prepositions to substitute for the noun which would appear after those prepositions in the sentence of which the *so*-clause is a permutation, e.g. *so tz'u* 所自 'that from which', 'whence' (for *tz'u* 自 in the sense of 'from' see note 280), *so yü* 所與 'the one with whom', *so wei* 所為 'the one on behalf of whom', 'that because of which', 'the reason why', and, most commonly, *so i* 所以 'the means whereby', 'the reason why'.

7. *yü* 於

yü 於 functions as a general-purpose preposition of location (meaning 'in', 'on', and 'at') and direction (meaning 'to', 'from', 'towards'). Thus we have so far met, for example, *yü kuo* 於國 'towards the state', *yü Ho-tung* 於河東 'to Ho-tung', *yü tao-lu* 於道路 'on the roads', *i yü* 異於 'different *from*', *yü t'ang shang* 於堂上 '*at* the top of the hall', *kao yü chün* 告於君 'report *to* a ruler', *yü wang ch'ien* 於王前 '*in* front of the king'. *hu* 乎 is also used occasionally in the same sense (see note 102).

The other usages of *yü* 於 are: (1) meaning 'in comparison with', 'than', it makes it necessary for the verb or adjective which precedes it to be translated in the comparative form, e.g. *to yü* 多於 means 'more numerous than'; (2) meaning 'by', it sometimes comes between verb and agent and shows that the verb should be translated in the passive—*ai yü jen* 愛於人 'to be loved by others' would be an example of this.

It is clear that these various 'meanings' of *yü* 於 are not meanings in the normal sense of the term. The *yü* 於 merely indicates the existence of a relationship of a vague locational or directional character, the precise nature of which is made clear by the context.

B. NEGATIVES

The most common negative is *pu* 不, which serves as an adverb to negate verbs, e.g. *pu jen* 不仁 'he does not behave humanely'. With nouns or adjectives it is the equivalent of our privative prefixes 'in-' or 'un-', e.g. *pu jen* 不仁 'inhumane', 'inhumanity'. The function of *pu* 不 is essentially the same in both these situations (cf. note 20).

The negative *wei* 未 similarly negates verbs, but by contrast with *pu* 不, which simply negates, the degree of generality or particularity coming from the context, *wei* 未 negates universally, meaning 'never' or 'not yet'. The 'never' may be temporal (e.g. *wei chien yang* 未見羊 'I never saw the sheep') or logical (e.g. *wei chih yu yeh* 未之有也 'it never is, could be, the case that . . .').

Neither *pu* 不 nor *wei* 未 have a positive antonym, but *wu* 無 'not have', 'lack', 'without', 'there are not' contrasts with *yu* 有 'to have', 'there are'. (Not surprisingly *pu yu* 不有 rarely occurs, and when it does there is a strong reason, e.g. the *pu* 不 may be part of a double negative such as *mo pu* 莫不, meaning 'everyone'.)

We have so far noticed *wu* 無 being used in the following ways: i. in the idiom *wu*—clause—*che* 無 . . . 者 'there are not those who . . .' or 'none', as contrasted with *yu*—clause—*che* 有 . . . 者 'there are those who . . .' or 'some' (see note 32 for an example); ii. as a main verb, e.g. *wu han* 無憾 'to lack resentment', *wu chi* 無饑 'be without hunger'; iii. as a privative, being equivalent to the suffix '-less', e.g. *wu shang* 無傷 'harmless'; iv. instead of the negative imperative adverb *wu* 毋 (see note 57).

By contrast with *pu* 不 and *wei* 未, which negate verbs (or nominalized verbs), *wu* 無 (naturally in view of its meaning) always goes with a noun/adjective (or, in the case of the *wu* . . . *che* 無 . . . 者 construction, a noun-clause), except of course when it stands for *wu* 毋. Most of the patterns in which *wu* 無 occurs have already been encountered and there should be no difficulty with it if the basic contrast with *yu* 有 is remembered.

Another important negative is *fei* 非, which is the negative proper to the non-verbal sentence. Thus *X fei Y yeh*, X 非 Y 也 means 'X is not Y'. Sometimes it negates what would otherwise appear to be a verbal sentence, but it does not simply negate the verb like *pu* 不, but negates or rejects the whole clause, i.e.

it is the negative of the explanatory clause terminating in *yeh* 也—'it is that', 'it is because', and means 'it is not the case that', e.g. *fei ai ch'i ts'ai erh i chih i yang yeh* 非愛其財而易之以羊也 'it is not the case that I exchanged it for a sheep because I begrudged the expense of it' (see note 101). Thus the whole explanation is rejected, and indeed the basic notion behind *fei* 非 is that of rejection. Its non-grammatical usages show this clearly. It often appears in contrast with *shih* 是 'this' (and hence 'the accepted', 'the right') in the sense of 'to reject' or 'to blame', or 'wrong' (i.e. meet to be rejected). *fei* 非 originated as a phonetic fusion of *pu* 不 with *wei* 唯, which in an earlier form of Chinese served as a copula.

The above four are the most common negatives, but the following have also been met and occur regularly: i. *mo* 莫, meaning 'nobody' or 'nothing' (see notes 76 and 152); ii. *fou* 否, which may be described as a proclausal negative, since it substitutes for a negative verbal clause or sentence ('No, I do not', 'or not'), as explained in note 121; iii. *wu* 勿, which probably stands for *wu chih* 毋之 (see note 57).

Note 185 will introduce us to *fu* 弗, another common negative.

C. FINAL PARTICLES

Apart from *yeh* 也 and *i* 矣 which have already been discussed, we have met *erh i (i)* 而已 (矣) 'and that's that', 'and that's all', which is discussed in note 11, and we have encountered two fusions of it, *erh* 耳 and *erh* 爾. We have also met the exclamatory final particle *tsai* 哉 a few times (see note 79). We have also encountered the quite common *yen* 焉, which stands for *yü chih* 於之, and *yü* 與 which, as a final particle, stands for *yeh hu* 也乎. The common interrogative final particle *hu* 乎 is discussed more appropriately in the next section.

D. INTERROGATIVES

We have noticed three different categories of interrogative: i. the formal interrogative, which presents a statement and asks whether it is true; ii. the material interrogative, which asks for new information; iii. the rhetorical interrogative, which is the equivalent of an exclamatory statement.

In the case of the formal interrogative the sentence appears in precisely the same order as the indicative statement, the only difference being that it is terminated with the particle *hu* 乎. There is no formal distinction between the wording of direct and indirect questions, as we noticed when discussing the alternative question *pu shih neng chih fou hu* 不識能至否乎 'I do not know whether he can have reached there or not' (see note 141). We have also met two fusion forms incorporating *hu* 乎, *chu* 諸 for *chih hu* 之乎 and *yü* 與 for *yeh hu* 也乎.

The material question is often formed with *ho* 何, which figures high in the list of most common characters. We have already met it with the following functions and meanings:

54

i. As interrogative adverb meaning 'why?', e.g. *wang ho pi yüeh li* 王何必曰利 'why must Your Majesty mention profit?'

ii. In the interrogative adverbial phrase *ho i* 何以 meaning 'by what means?', 'how?', e.g. *ho i li wu kuo* 何以利吾國 'how shall I profit my state?'

iii. Meaning 'why?' but forming the predicate of a non-verbal sentence, i.e. 'X is why?' meaning 'why is it that X?' (see note 34).

iv. As interrogative pronoun 'what?', e.g. *te ho ju* 德何如, literally 'if one's virtue is like what?', i.e. 'with what sort of virtue?' (see note 75).

v. In the idiom *ho ju* 何如 'what would that be like?', 'what would you think of that?'

vi. In the idiom *ju chih ho* 如之何 'in such circumstances why?'

vii. In *ho yu* 何由 'from what?', 'whence?'

viii. With a verb of motion as interrogative adverb 'where?', e.g. *niu ho chih* 牛何之 'where is the ox going?' (This is really 'what is the ox going to?' and so could be included under iv.)

ix. As an interrogative adjective 'what?', e.g. *shih ch'eng ho hsin tsai* 是誠何心哉, literally 'this is really what mind?', i.e. 'what really are my motives in this?' The *ho* 何 again comes as in iii, in the predicate of a non-verbal sentence.

x. in *ho tsai* 何哉, an exclamatory 'what!'

The range is wide, and the points to notice are (1) that in a non-verbal sentence the *ho* 何 comes in the predicate; (2) that there is a natural tendency for the *ho* 何 to adopt a position in the sentence which would be occupied by the answering word given in reply to the *ho* 何. Thus when it means 'how?' it takes the adverbial position, and when it means 'what?' or 'what sort of?' it takes the adjectival position. An exception to this is that if it is the object of a verb (e.g. in *ho ju* 何如) or verb-preposition (e.g. in *ho i* 何以) it precedes the verb or verb-preposition.

Other material interrogative words, which have only occurred once each so far, are *wu* 惡 'how?', *hsi* 奚 'what?', and *yen* 焉 (related to final particle *yen* 焉) 'in what?', 'where?', 'in what respect?', 'how?'

The latter was encountered in combination with the exclamatory final particle *tsai* 哉 to form a rhetorical question (see note 131). We have also met one example of the rhetorical interrogative *ch'i* 豈 'how?', 'surely not?' (see note 149).

E. AUXILIARY VERBS

These can be treated in two groups: a. those which give some indication of the time of the action of the verb; b. others.

a. Temporal auxiliaries are used rarely, for the time of the action is usually either self-evident from the context or irrelevant, e.g. in passage A we can translate *ho i li wu kuo* 何以利吾國 as 'how do I profit my kingdom?' or 'how shall I profit my kingdom?', for the tense we give to the question is immaterial. In the five passages we have read we have only met nine occurrences of a temporal auxiliary. The most common of these temporal auxiliaries in Mencius is *chiang*

將 'to be about to', which may provide a simple future (e.g. *chiang i hsin chung* 將以釁鍾 'we are about to consecrate a bell with it') or may be set in the past (e.g. *Lu P'ing kung chiang ch'u* 魯平公將出 'Duke P'ing of Lu *was* about to go out').

We have also met two auxiliaries which indicate that the action of the verb is completed, *i* 已, literally 'to finish', and therefore commonly translatable as 'have finished', 'have already', 'have', and *chi* 既 which is used in a similar way in, e.g., *ping jen chi chieh* 兵刃既接 'when the weapon blades have clashed'.

It is obviously inappropriate to talk in terms of tense or aspect when discussing these auxiliaries because both these concepts imply systems in which tense or aspect are expressed as essential elements in the verb-form, so that every time the verb occurs it has tense or aspect. What we have here is a small group of words which have developed grammatical functions of this kind out of their ordinary non-grammatical meanings, but which never become so institutionalized that they develop into essential features of the verb form.

b. We have also met various auxiliaries indicating ability, possibility, etc. and should attempt to distinguish between them:

i. *neng* 能 is 'to be able', 'to have the ability to'.

ii. *tsu i* 足以 is somewhat similar but, since *tsu* 足 by itself means 'sufficient', it means 'to have the capacity to', 'to be adequate to', and, more often than *neng* 能, is found with non-personal subjects, e.g. *shih hsin tsu i wang i* 是心足以王矣 'this heart is adequate for kingship'. *tsu i* 足以 is always followed by an active verb; before a passive verb (that is to say, a verb not followed by an object) we find *tsu* by itself, as in *tsu yü yen* 足與言 'fit to be conversed with' (see note 150).

iii. *ko i* 可以 means 'to be able to' in the sense that the circumstances are suitable, not that one has the innate ability (which is indicated by *neng* 能), e.g. *wu shih che k'o i i po i* 五十者可以衣帛矣 'fifty-year-olds may, will be able to, wear silk (because the circumstances are favourable)' or, to give a translation which makes the contrast with *neng* 能 absolutely clear, 'it will become possible for fifty-year-olds to wear silk'. *k'o i* 可以, as explained in note 55, always goes with an active verb. Before a passive verb we find *k'o* 可 by itself, e.g. *k'o fei* 可廢 'may be dispensed with'. The senses of permissibility ('may') or propriety ('should') are sometimes present.

iv. *te* 得, which means 'to get', also functions as an auxiliary verb meaning 'to be able to' in the sense of 'to get to', 'to manage to', 'to succeed in'.

We also noticed two idiomatic expressions which should be mentioned here: *pu k'o sheng* 不可勝 'cannot exhaustively' (see note 49); and *pu te i* 不得已 or *ju pu te i* 如不得已 'if one cannot avoid it', 'having no alternative' (see note 143).

Another common auxiliary verb which we have met a few times is *pi* 必, which means 'must', 'to be bound to', but which it is sometimes better to treat as an adverb and translate as 'always' or 'invariably'. In such contexts there is no suggestion of necessity in the meaning of the word.

Auxiliary verbs meaning 'wish to' (*yü* 欲 and *yüan* 願) and 'dare to' (*kan* 敢) will be met later.

F. How Clauses are Interrelated

We have already dealt with *erh* 而, which serves as a kind of general-purpose conjunction between clauses. Another very common conjunction linking subordinate and main clause is *tse* 則 'then', which may come after what the context reveals to be either a conditional, temporal, or causal clause—'if . . . then . . .', 'when . . . then . . .', 'since . . . then . . .'. As we have seen, in most cases the subordinate clause has to be translated as an 'if' clause. We have also met examples of *tse* 則 preceded by a single word, rather than by a clause (see note 144). The conjunction *ssu* 斯 'then' is used in much the same way as *tse* 則 but is far less common, and *chi* 即 also functions in the same way in certain authors.

Although the protasis is not usually introduced by a word meaning 'if,' there are several words which occasionally perform such a function, some of which we have already met. The most common is *ju* 如, which gives a remote flavour to the condition (*wang ju chih tz'u* 王如知此 'if Your Majesty were to understand this'). *jo* 若 also means 'if,' and we must not forget that both *ju* 如 and *jo* 若 also function as verbs or verb-prepositions meaning 'to be like', 'to do like', 'like'. We have also met *kou* 苟 (*kou wei hou i* 苟爲後義 'if you are reputed to put justice last'). If the protasis is introduced by a word meaning 'if', it may or may not have a *tse* 則 linking it with the apodosis. Often, too, the mere juxtaposition of clauses is sufficient to indicate a conditional relationship without assistance from function words.

The proclausal *jan* 然 (= *ju chih* 如之) substitutes for an if-clause understood from the previous context, meaning 'if that is so'. It is sometimes linked with the main clause by means of a *tse* 則 or an *erh* 而. (We have also met *jan* 然 as a verb meaning 'to be so' or 'to do so' and as an adverbial suffix equivalent to '-ly'.)

The causal relationship between clauses is generally indicated by linking them by means of *ku* 故, *shih i* 是以, or *shih ku* 是故, all meaning 'therefore' or 'that is why'. We have had examples of the first two of these. *i* 亦 'also' sometimes appears to have a similar function, but what is said in note 4 should be remembered.

The concessive relationship is generally indicated by means of *sui* 雖 'although' introducing the concessive clause, and we have already had an example of this.

Normally words like *ju* 如, *jo* 若 and *sui* 雖, when introducing a subordinate clause, follow the subject of the clause, as for example in *wang ju chih tz'u* 王如知此 quoted above.

The conjunctions mentioned in this section are all subordinating conjunctions. Conjunctions which serve to link co-ordinate clauses are much rarer, but see notes 218, 284, and 315 for *ch'ieh* 且, *yu* 又 and *sui* 遂, which perform this function.

G. Miscellaneous

Here is a brief reminder of some of the other categories of grammatical words and forms that we have already encountered:

i. Demonstratives: *shih* 是 and *tz'u* 此 'this'; *pi* 彼 'that'.

ii. Personal pronouns. In addition to *chih* 之 we have met the third person possessive pronoun *ch'i* 其 ('his', 'her', 'its', 'their') and the first person pronouns *wo* 我, *wu* 吾, and *yü* 予. As compared with *wo* 我, which may occur in any position, *wu* 吾 appears only as subject or possessive pronoun ('I' or 'my') or as pre-verbal object in a negative sentence. *yü* 予 is archaic. So far we have had no instance of the second person pronouns. These are uncommon because people are generally addressed in the third person, as e.g. *wang* 王, *tzu* 子, *chün* 君, with the third person possessive and objective pronouns *ch'i* 其 and *chih* 之 being used where appropriate.

iii. Prepositions and Postpositions.

a. Prepositions. In addition to the common general-purpose *yü* 於 we nave also met *yu* 由 'from', *wei* 為 'because of', 'on behalf of', and *yü* 與 'together with'.

b. Postpositions: *shang* 上 'above', and *hsia* 下 'below'.

PASSAGE F

A conversation between Mo-tzu and Wu Lü in which the former argues that preaching is more beneficial than merely practising (from *Mo-tzu*, ch. 49).

158.   *tzu* 自 is used commonly as a pronominal adverb, which often provides the equivalent of our reflexive pronoun 'himself', as here—'he compared himself'. Sometimes, however, it is used not reflexively but in emphasis of the subject— 'he *himself*', 'he personally'.

It also occurs as a preposition meaning 'from'.

159.   The first *tzu* 子 qualifies the *Mo-tzu* 墨子 and the word order is the same as in the English translation: 'our master Mo-tzu'.

160.   The interrogative expression *yen yung* 焉用 means literally 'used for what?' It is equivalent to the English expression 'what is the use of?', the rhetorical nature of the question being reinforced by the presence of the exclamatory particle *tsai* 哉.

161.   Here we have an example of the purposive *i* 以—'wherewith to', 'in order to'.

162.   For *fen jen* 分人 one might have expected *fen yü jen* 分於人 'divide among men', but the parallelism with *lao jen* 勞人 is retained. There is a tendency for *yü* 於 to drop out in this way when the meaning is clear without it. *Mo-tzu* is, however, an imperfectly preserved text, and one cannot be sure that the *yü* 於 did not drop out during transmission.

163.   Here in the usual way Mo-tzu refers to himself by name instead of using a first person pronoun.

164.   *ch'ang* 嘗, which means 'to taste', 'to experience', consequently occurs as a temporal auxiliary indicating that the action of the verb has been experienced and is therefore in the past. As compared with *i* 已 and *chi* 既, which mean that the action of the verb is over and done with, *ch'ang* 嘗 dwells on the experience and means that the action of the verb has happened at some time or other in the past. 'Once' is often the best translation: 'I once contemplated'. Except when it occurs in its non-grammatical meaning of 'to taste', *ch'ang* 嘗 is never negated by *pu* 不, but always by *wei* 未, naturally since the negative of 'I once contemplated' is 'I never at any time contemplated'.

165.   *shih* 食 normally means 'to eat', but here the verb is used causatively— 'to cause to eat', i.e. 'to feed'. In this sense it is pronounced *ssu*.

166.   *jan hou* 然後, literally 'it being so, consequently', means 'only in such circumstances', 'then and only then'. Often it can be most neatly translated by

introducing the preceding clause with the words 'only if': thus in the present passage, '*only if* it were successful, would I take on the ploughing of a single farmer'.

167.   Here is a case of *chu* 諸 standing for *chih yü* 之於. Thus on this occasion, as compared with the previous *fen jen* 分人, the text does have a word for 'among' after the *fen* 分.

168.   A use of *neng* 能 where one might have expected *k'o i* 可以. The context is very similar to the places in passage B where *k'o i* 可以 occurs (cf. note 55 and Grammatical Survey E[b]).

169.   Here *jen* 人 appears unusually in an adverbial position meaning 'individually'. The *te* 得 of course functions here as a main verb in the sense of 'to get', not as an auxiliary.

170.   Notice the formula for expressing quantities in *i sheng su* 一升粟 'a *sheng* of grain', with the word expressing quantity coming between the number and the noun.

171.   *chieh* 藉 means 'to rely on', 'to avail oneself of'. Here in *chieh erh* 藉而 we have a related grammatical usage 'availing oneself of the idea that', i.e. 'supposing that'.

172.   Compare the construction of this sentence with its English equivalent. We would want to start with 'it is already obvious that' (*k'o tu* 可睹—'may be observed', 'observable', 'obvious'), but the Chinese puts the that-clause first. The *ch'i* 其 fulfils the function normally performed by noun + *chih* 之 in forming a noun clause—'their not being able' or 'the fact that they are not able'.

173.   It looks as if an *i* 一 may have dropped out before the *ch'ih pu* 尺布, which one would expect to balance the earlier *i sheng su* 一斤粟.

174.   This expression *chu hou* 諸侯 'the feudal lords' is very common. The *chu* 諸 means 'all', 'the various', but it becomes so absorbed in the total meaning of the expression that *chu hou* 諸侯 can even be used to refer to *one* feudal lord. The collective prefix *chu* 諸 is normally to be found only with one of a small number of nouns denoting classes of people, e.g. *ch'en* 臣 'ministers', *tai-fu* 大夫 'grandees', *tzu* 子 'sons'.

175.   The fact that there is no *che* 者 after the *san chün* 三軍 shows that in the previous sentences one should not take the *ches* 者 as clause-terminators, but as going only with the *chi* 饑 and the *han* 寒, i.e. *chi che* 饑者 'those who are hungry', 'the hungry', *han che* 寒者 'those who are cold', 'the cold'.

176.   *pu jo* 不若 is an idiom meaning 'there is nothing like', 'the best thing is to'. *pu ju* 不如 also occurs in the same sense. The idiom is intelligible if one understands a subject of the *pu jo* 不若, e.g. '*these proposals* are not like, not as good as reciting . . .', so 'the best thing is to recite . . .'.

177.   Here the text has an incomplete series, for after *shang* 上 'first' and *tz'u* 次 'next' *hsia* 下 'last' would normally be expected. It is fairly clear that

something has dropped out. Note this new use of *shang* 上 and *hsia* 下. They are used to mean 'first' and 'second' of a set of two. Similarly *shang* 上, *chung* 中, and *hsia* 下 mean 'first', 'second', and 'third' of three.

178.　　This *chih* 治 illustrates that when a verb does not govern an object and is therefore not active, it may often be treated either as a passive verb or as a stative verb-adjective. This distinction can be shown in English by contrasting 'is well governed' or 'is being governed well' (passive) and 'is well-governed' (stative).

179.　　Starting here we have a rather complicated sentence 28 characters long. A lengthy concessive clause separates the *i wei* 以為 from the clause dependent upon it, whose verb is *hsien* 賢. Finally the *yü* 於 'than' leads into a long substantival clause terminated by *che* 者.

180.　　*she* 設 means 'to establish' and, as a grammatical word, it is used to introduce a conditional clause with the sense 'supposing'. Here *chieh she erh* 藉設而 is used in the same way as *chieh erh* 藉而 (see note 171).

181.　　Here for the first time we meet the interrogative pronoun *shu* 孰 'which?' The Chinese equivalent of 'which out of X and Y is the greater?' is X *yü* Y *shu ta* X 與 Y 孰大. But here we have something more complicated: 'of the achievements of X and Y which is the greater?' Notice that instead of linking the long *che*-clause with *kung* 功 directly by means of the possessive *chih* 之 it is felt necessary to resume the whole of the *che*-clause by means of the possessive pronoun *ch'i* 其. Similarly we might say 'As for X and Y, which of them is the more meritorious?'

　　shu 孰 never occurs as object.

182.　　Note that, as a general rule, *shao* 少 'few' does not appear in the adjectival position qualifying the object, even when it relates closely to the object. Instead it occupies the adverbial position. Thus 'gave him few weapons' would be *shao yü chih ping* 少與之兵, literally 'sparsely gave him weapons'. In the present context we should translate 'understand little (about) righteousness'. The same rule also applies to *to* 多 'many'.

183.　　Here instead of a double object after the verb *chiao* 教 'to teach', as in the English 'to teach the world righteousness', we have the thing taught introduced by the verb-preposition *i* 以, i.e. 'to teach the world *using/by means c,* righteousness'.

184.　　The expression *ho ku* 何故 'for what reason?', 'why?' provides another example of *ho* 何 as interrogative adjective.

185.　　*fu* 弗 is a negative we have not met before. It probably stands for *pu chih* 不之, just as *wu* 勿 probably stands for *wu chih* 毋之. It may not be obvious who is the subject of *fu yen* 弗言, but if we refer back to the *yen yung yen chih tsai* 焉用言之哉 near the beginning of the passage (54 i–m) we see that this is a direct reply to that and must be in the first person—'why should I not talk about it?'

186.　　This is an instance of the use of *te* 得 as an auxiliary verb—'to succeed in', 'to manage to', 'to be able to'.

187.　　Here we have the rhetorical *ch'i* 豈 succeeded by *pu* 不, the sentence being terminated by *tsai* 哉. *ch'i pu* 豈不 means 'surely not not', i.e. with the two negatives cancelling each other out 'surely' or 'how not?'

188.　　*i* 益 'increasingly', 'more', like *chia* 加 (see note 33), provides a way of forming a comparative.

PASSAGE G

Mo-tzu disapproves of the inventor Kung-shu P'an for placing his 'cloud-ladders' at the disposal of Ch'u to attack Sung, since Ch'u already has abundant territory (from *Mo-tzu*, ch. 50).

189.　　Duration of time is commonly rendered in this way, the time being stated plainly without preposition at the end of the clause, whereas we normally say '*for* ten days and nights'. Sometimes, however, the period of time is thought of as affecting the quality of the action of the verb and it therefore appears in the adverbial position, e.g. *san nien hsüeh* 三年學 'to study for three years' (in Analects VIII. 12), which means much the same as 'to study diligently'.

190.　　*fu-tzu* 夫子 is a more honorific form of address than plain *tzu* 子 ('Confucius' is a Latinization of *K'ung-fu-tzu* 孔夫子, K'ung being his surname). *fu* 夫 we have already met as a noun in *i-fu* 一夫 and *tai-fu* 大夫. As a grammatical word it functions as a kind of mild demonstrative, often not needing translation but placing emphasis on the noun that follows it (see note 206).

191.　　In this sentence the speaker refers both to himself and to his interlocutor in the third person—'what does the Master order this person to do?' Similarly in his reply Mo-tzu refers to himself in the third person as *ch'en* 臣 'your servant', and his interlocutor as *tzu* 子. *ming* 命 'to order' is generally followed directly by the person ordered without the preposition *yü* 於 (as, e.g., at 34 s–u), but cf. note 116 for a similar unexpected use of *yen* 焉.

192.　　There appears to be a *che* 者 missing from the end of this clause. Without it one would have to take *wu* 侮 adjectivally—'in the north there is an *insulting* servant', but what we need is 'in the north there is *one who insults* your servant'.

193.　　This character *shuo* 說 is often written in ancient texts as a loan for *yüeh* 悅 'to be pleased'. Only the context will tell which of the two interpretations is correct. Although either interpretation might seem possible here, the formula X *pu yüeh* X 不悅 after a speech by Y is very common, so that is how it should be taken. In the next line, however, it clearly cannot be read *yüeh*. Some inconsistency in the use of radicals is a feature of the texts of this period.

194.　　Notice the role of *ku* 固 before a negative as an intensifier—'certainly will not', 'absolutely refuse to'.

195.   Here we meet the preposition *ts'ung* 從 'from', which functions in the same way as *yu* 由, i.e. in the pattern *ts'ung*-noun-verb (see note 115). The unusual feature here is that the verb is not a verb of motion.

ts'ung 從 is also used as a verb meaning 'to follow'.

196.   In *tzu wei t'i* 子為梯 the normal *chih* 之 and *yeh* 也 of reported speech are omitted and, as is the case with questions, there is no formal distinction between the direct and the indirect.

197.   *ho tsui chih yu* 何罪之有 is an example of an idiom which does not occur in Mencius but is met frequently in the *Tso-chuan*. *ho X chih yu* 何 X 之有 means 'what X is there?' or 'what X does (it) possess?' *yu ho X* 有何 X ('there is what X?') would seem to be the natural Chinese construction here, but instead the *ho X* 何 X is reinforced with an anaphoric *chih* 之; rather as we might say, 'What guilt is it that (Sung) possesses?' instead of simply 'what guilt does (Sung) possess?'

198.   It is clear that the *so* 所 here is used where one might expect *so yü* 所於, which in fact never occurs. Just previously the text reads *pu tsu yü min* 不足於民, literally 'is inadequate in population', so the *so*-clause referring back to that must mean 'to kill *that in which* it is inadequate', viz. population. *so* 所 often occurs for *so yü* 所於 in this way, and it should be noted that *so pu tsu* 所不足 cannot mean 'that which is inadequate', since *so* 所 is never the subject of the *so*-clause. Similarly *so yu yü* 所有餘 means 'that in which they have a surplus', referring back to *yu yü yü ti* 有餘於地 'have a surplus in territory'.

199.   The construction of this clause is difficult. One has to understand a *sha* 殺 after the *shao* 少, remembering the rule about *shao* 少 stated in note 182. The translation is 'in killing it is righteous not to kill a few, but to kill many'.

PASSAGE H

CONFUCIUS, accompanied by his disciples Yen Hui and Tzu Kung, calls on Robber Chih' (beginning of *Chuang-tzu*, ch. 29).

200.   Notice that *yü* 與 can here be regarded as either a conjunction or a preposition. The sentence may be translated either 'Confucius *and* Liu-hsia Chi were friends' or 'Confucius was friends *with* Liu-hsia Chi'.

201.   *ming yüeh* 名曰 means 'was called'. The *yüeh* 曰 does not need translating, for it often merely plays the part of inverted commas.

202.   Notice the word order here. Instead of saying 'the Brigand Chih had nine thousand followers', the normal word-order is as here: 'the followers (of) the Brigand Chih (were) nine thousand men'. Notice also the complete lack of grammatical words in this sentence.

203.   Notice that there is no possessive *chih* 之 after the *jen* 人. This makes possible the retention of the four-character pattern.

204.   Here for the first time we have a case of a *so*-clause qualifying a noun—'the cities which he passed'.

205.   *wan* 萬 'ten thousand' comes to be used in the sense of 'all of the numerous'. Thus *wan wu* 萬物, 'the ten thousand things', is a very common expression meaning 'everything'. *wan min* 萬民 occurs occasionally in the sense of 'all the people'.

206.   *fu* 夫 preceding a noun places a slight emphasis on it, and is very often used when a piece of new subject matter is introduced. The word 'now' in English is sometimes used in the same manner and will often prove a satisfactory translation. Sometimes a demonstrative will serve the purpose. See note 190 for other uses of *fu* 夫.

207.   When a generalization about fatherhood is made the expressions *wei jen fu* 為人父 'to be a father' and *wei jen fu che* 為人父者 'fathers' sometimes occur. Inherent in the *wei* 為 is the sense of 'to act as', 'to play the part of', so perhaps 'those who fulfil the role of fathers' gets nearest to the sense. The *jen* 人 in the expression (as also in *jen chün* 人君—'a ruler') seems superfluous, but presumably the meaning is 'father of men', 'ruler of men'.

208.   *jo* 若 here makes the condition remote—'should fathers . . .', 'if fathers were to . . .'. It is unusual for *jo* 若 meaning 'if' to precede the subject of the if-clause. The reason why it does so here is that it has to go with two parallel clauses and, if it had appeared after the *fu* 父, it would have been necessary to repeat it after the *hsiung* 兄.

209.   This 无 is the way in which *wu* 無 is written in the text of Chuang-tzu.

210.   Notice the effect on the meaning of *wu* 无 caused by the presence of *i* 矣 at the end of the sentence. It gives a sense of the momentary to a verb which of its own nature is concerned with lasting states rather than momentary events; in other words it comes to mean 'cease to exist'. The sense of the passage can best be brought out in English by 'there would be an end to the value attached to . . .'.

211.   Notice the adverb-verb compound noun *hsien-sheng* 先生, literally 'previously born', and therefore 'senior'. It is used as a respectful term of address.

212.   The presence of *shih* 世 in the expression *shih chih ts'ai shih* 世之才士 'talented scholar of the age' has the effect of making the expression into a kind of superlative, and it would be quite proper to translate it as 'the most talented scholar of the age'. The use of *t'ien hsia* 天下 instead of *shih* 世 would have a similar effect.

213.   In this and the preceding sentences there are two 'copulas', but one is expressed by *yeh* 也 and the other by *wei* 為. There is a subtle difference between the two, *wei* 為 always having something of the flavour of either 'become' or 'play the part of', or, in other words, reference to *being at a particular time* rather than without any temporal reference. Again, in the next sentence *wei* 為

64

in *wei t'ien-hsia hai* 為天下害 is something like 'constitutes' or 'has become' rather than a completely colourless 'is'. Earlier we had *wei jen fu che* 為人父者 and there again the sentence only made sense if *wei* 為 contained some suggestion of 'really playing the part of', for something more than the completely colourless copula was demanded by the context.

214.　　A good example of *fu* 弗 = *pu chih* 不之 (cf. note 185).

215.　　*ch'ieh* 竊, whose non-grammatical sense is 'steal', 'stealthy', has a quasi-grammatical usage here in that it imparts a deferential tone to the statement, the meaning 'humbly' being obviously related to 'stealthily'. The *wei* 為 after it is the preposition, meaning 'on behalf of'.

216.　　Here we have *sui* 雖 going with a noun rather than a clause and therefore meaning 'even'—'even your present eloquence'.

217.　　*nai ho* 奈何 in Chuang-tzu means the same as *ju chih ho* 如之何 in Mencius (see note 138). The *nai chih ho* 奈之何 which occurs here comes no-where else in the book so the *chih* 之 is probably an interpolation. *ju chih ho* 如之何 never occurs in Chuang-tzu. It would therefore seem likely that *nai* 奈 is a phonetic fusion of *ju chih* 如之, especially as this conclusion is supported by other evidence and seems possible according to experts' opinion on how these words were pronounced in antiquity. The temporal auxiliary *chiang* 將 often appears in conjunction with this idiom, with verb understood—'what will you (do) in such circumstances?'

218.　　*ch'ieh* 且 has two grammatical functions: (1) as here, as a coordinate conjunction between clauses—'and', 'moreover'; (2) as a temporal auxiliary rather like *chiang* 將—'be about to'. As a conjunction it never links nouns, this function being performed where necessary by *yü* 與 or *chi* 及.

219.　　The idiom X *chih wei jen yeh* X 之為人也 is a common introduction to a description of a man's character. In form the idiom looks like a case of the use of *yeh* 也 to expose elements in the sentence for the sake of emphasis—'as for X's being a man, he . . . .'. It is tantamount to a reply to the question X *ho jen yeh* X 何人也 'what sort of a man is X?' Obviously X *chih jen yeh* X 之人也 would not do for 'as for X's being a man . . .' or 'X is such a man that . . .', because a verb is needed to complete the noun-*chih*-verb-noun-*yeh* formula, so that seems to be why the *wei* 為 is included in spite of the fact that the use of *wei* 為 as copula does not have the same meaning as the copula in the X Y *yeh* formula (cf. note 213). In later Chinese the *chih* 之 and *yeh* 也 are commonly omitted from the formula.

220.　　An example of *fei* 非 occurring not as a negative, but with the meaning 'wrong'.

221.　　Notice that the negative *wu* 无 is used after *pi* 必 in the sense of 'must not'.

222.　　On these uses of *wei* 為 cf. note 213.

223.   The grammatical usages of *fang* 方 (which also has several non-grammatical senses) have to do with coincidence in time. Sometimes it introduces a clause and means 'while', 'so long as', 'at the moment when'; but sometimes, as here, it occupies an adverbial position and means 'just at that moment'.

224.   *nai* 乃 is a difficult word to translate because it has several different functions although it is not common. One of its meanings is 'actually', 'really' (cf. note 103) and here I think it should be taken in that sense but closely with the *fang* 方—'just at that moment'.

225.   Notice the verb-object compound noun *chiang-chün* 將軍 'general' (cf. note 108).

226.   Here the *fu* 夫 may conveniently be translated as demonstrative—'that'.

227.   Notice that here we have *fei* 非 meaning 'or not' rather than *fou* 否. This is because the construction is non-verbal, and *fou* 否 goes with verbal sentences.

228.   *yeh* 邪 is in certain authors used to write the phonetic fusion of *yeh hu* 也乎, which, as we have noticed, is written *yü* 與 in Mencius (see note 87).

229.   *erh* 爾, which we have met before standing for *erh i* 而已 (see note 151), here means 'you'. It is the first time we have encountered a second person pronoun: Brigand Chih is rather rude to use it instead of a polite form of address such as *hsien-sheng* 先生.

230.   Here is a case of *to* 多 appearing in the adverbial position, but really relating to the object of the verb, just like the example of *shao* 少 explained in note 182.

231.   Here we have a case of *shih* 是 and *fei* 非 contrasted in the sense of 'right' and 'wrong'.

232.   Note that instead of 'add A to B', the idiom here is 'augment B by means of (*i* 以) A'.

233.   Here even *liang* 兩 'two' appears in the adverbial position in the manner of *shao* 少 and *to* 多 (see notes 182 and 230).

234.   Here we have, as often, an adverbial phrase without preposition where we need to supply one—'with a sound like a tigress with young'.

235.   Another example of the *wen chih* 聞之 idiom (see note 82).

236.   *fan* 凡 means 'all' and precedes the noun it qualifies. As compared with *chu* 諸 (see note 174), which tends to occur in certain set phrases like *chu hou* 諸侯, its use is not restricted to any particular set of nouns and it often qualifies substantival clauses: e.g. *fan wo t'ung meng chih jen* 凡我同盟之人 'all we who have sworn together' (*Mencius* VIb. 7).

237.   *chieh* 皆, on the other hand, never precedes the noun in the manner of *chu* 諸 and *fan* 凡. It may appear immediately after a subject (in the same sense as 'men *all* . . .' as cf. 'all men') or it may appear independently but

agreeing with the subject, as in the present context. Cases do occur of it appearing in the adverbial position but relating to the object of the verb, in exactly the same way as *to* 多 and *shao* 少, e.g. *ti chieh tse chih* 狄皆則之, 'the barbarians copy all these' (*Tso-chuan*, Duke Hsi, year 24). See note 90 for an earlier occurrence of this word.

238.　　Here is an instance of *shang, chung,* and *hsia* 上中下 being used to mean first, second, and third of a group of three (cf. note 177).

239.　　*chu* 諸 generally qualifies groups of people, e.g. *chu hou* 諸侯, *chu ch'en* 諸臣, *chu tai-fu* 諸大夫, and this is the only instance in *Chuang-tzu* of it coming with *wu* 物.

240.　　Be careful to avoid the trap of translating 'all men who . . .', as if the *fan jen* 凡人 were subject of the *che*-clause. This is, of course, impossible since the *che* 者 itself makes what precedes act as the subject of the sentence. The correct translation is 'among all mankind those who . . .'. 'All men who have X' would be *fan yu* X *chih jen* 凡有X之人 (cf. note 236).

241.　　Notice the construction of *tz'u i te* 此一德. It does not mean 'this one virtue'. It stands for *tz'u chih i te* 此之一德 and means 'one virtue of these', 'one of these virtues'.

242.　　Here we have a case of *che* 者 after a numeral, *san che* 三者 meaning 'these three things'.

243.　　Whereas we would say 'you are eight feet two inches *tall*', the Chinese equivalent has the word for tall before the measurement—'your body is *tall* eight feet two inches'. This is the form in which measurements and areas are commonly given. e.g. *fang ssu shih li* 方四十里 means 'forty li *square*'.

244.　　Here *shih* 使 is used in two different senses in quick succession: (1) in the passive—'to be sent'. In this sense it appears in a string of four parallel clauses in which it should be observed that the *nan* 南, *pei* 北, *tung* 東, and *hsi* 西 occupy the adverbial position, leaving the postverbal position clear for the destination place-names; and (2) 'to cause', 'to bring it about that'. The verb *tsao* 造 'to create', with no subject expressed, is dependent upon this *shih* 使 and, as often when no subject is expressed, is more easily translated with the aid of a passive—'cause there to be created'.

245.　　Note that expressions of area or extent come in this form, immediately after the noun to which they refer—*ta ch'eng shu pai li* 大城數百里 is 'a great wall of several hundred li' (cf. note 243).

246.　　Notice the use of *wei* 為 to mean 'as' in the construction 'to honour A *as* B'. The construction is similar to that of the *i* X *wei* Y 以X為Y idiom, and the meaning of *wei* 為 here derives naturally from its ordinary verbal meaning.

247.　　Here is a case of *chu hou* 諸侯 in the singular, referring to one feudal lord although *chu* 諸 means 'all' (see note 174).

248.   It is most unusual to find *erh* 而 linking the predicates of a non-verbal sentence, as it does here.

PASSAGE I

THE notorious Li Chi, concubine of Duke Hsien, who ruled over the state of Chin in the middle of the seventh century B.C., plots the downfall of Shen-sheng, the heir to the throne (from *Kuo-yü, Chin-yü*).

249.   Li Chi is the subject of this verb. It is an abrupt change of subject, but it presents no problem when one is familiar with the story.

250.   When *chieh* 皆, which normally means 'all', is associated with a dual subject it must of course be translated 'both'—'both of these have . . .' or here better 'in both of these there are . . .'.

251.   In *yu so hsing chih* 有所行之 we have a *so*-clause with object. In such cases (unless the verb is one which takes a double object, e.g. *wei* 謂 'to call') the *so* 所 is substituting for the purpose-clause which could follow the object in the simple verbal sentence of which the *so*-clause is a permutation. Purpose clauses without an introductory word meaning 'in order to' occur after appropriate verbs such as *hsing* 行 and *yung* 用. We can imagine a simple verbal sentence *Shen-sheng hsing chih* 申生行之 followed by a verb—'Shen-sheng is doing this to bring about so-and-so'. The cognate *so*-clause here means 'in both of these there is that for which he is doing them', i.e. 'both of these have some purpose'.

252.   *chün* 君 is used frequently in this passage as a quasi-pronoun of the second person.

253.   This is our first example of *yü* 於 meaning 'by', introducing the agent and converting the verb which precedes it into the passive.

254.   *wu nai* 無乃 'is it not the case that?', 'surely', introduces a rhetorical question or strongly affirmative statement. Sentences introduced by *wu nai* 無乃 often terminate with *hu* 乎.

255.   *i kuo ku* 以國故 means 'for the sake of the state'. *i*—phrase or clause—*ku* 以 . . . 故 becomes a common construction in Han Chinese meaning 'because of . . .'.

256.   In *Kuo-yü* and *Tso-chuan ch'i* 其 sometimes acts as a temporal auxiliary indicating that the action of the verb is in the future. It often occurs in questions or commands, but sometimes also in indicative sentences. Here, as often with the *jo chih ho* 若之何 or *ju chih ho* 如之何 idioms, there is no main verb expressed (cf. *chiang nai ho* 將奈何, note 217). The meaning is 'in such circumstances what will you (do)?'

257.   *ho* 盍 is an interrogative adverb which is thought to be a phonetic fusion of *ho pu* 何不 'why not?' An alternative way of writing this is *kai* 蓋. *ho* 盍 and *kai* 蓋 share the same phonetic and in ancient times they were pro-

nounced alike, with a final -p sound, which makes the fusion phonologically credible.

258. The clause beginning with *wu* 無 is a purpose clause without introductory grammatical word. *wu* 無 needs to be given a more forceful meaning than usual—'to do without', 'to avoid', i.e. 'to avoid throwing the people into confusion because of a single concubine'.

259. *fu* 夫 here occurs as a demonstrative but not, as usual, adjectivally: instead it functions as a pronoun, meaning 'this person', 'he'.

260. Another instance of the *wen chih* 聞之 idiom (see note 82).

261. There is a zeugma here: *wei jen* 爲仁 means 'to *practise* humaneness' and *wei kuo* 爲國 'to *run* a state'.

262. Here the verb *wei* 謂 takes two objects, *ai ch'in* 愛親 and *jen* 仁, the *ai ch'in* 愛親 being immediately referred back to by the pronoun *chih* 之. The effect is to place an emphasis on the *ai ch'in* 愛親 which may be rendered by translating the sentence: 'loving parents (or "kinsfolk")—it is this that people call humanity'. The usage of *chih* 之 is similar to that of *shih* 是 in the *Kuo-yü* and *Tso-chuan* described in note 266; cf. also note 197. Note 304 discusses an occurrence of *wei chih* 謂之 in the normal verb-object order.

263. For the sake of emphasis the *chung* 衆 is here placed in front of the *i* 以 instead of behind it—'it is the masses he treats as his kin'.

264. Another example of *i* . . . *ku* 以 . . . 故 (see note 255).

265. *k'uang* 況 is an interrogative adverb meaning 'how much the more?' and thus introducing a rhetorical question. Sometimes it is followed by *yü* X 於 X to mean 'how much the more is this so in the case of X?'

266. This usage of *shih* 是, which also occurs commonly in the *Tso-chuan*, enables emphasis to be placed on the object of the sentence. The word order of this sentence-pattern is object—*shih* 是—verb. Thus in the present context the word-for-word translation is 'all the people's advantage—this it produces', i.e. 'it is the advantage of all the people that it produces'. In other words *fan min li* 凡民利 is the grammatical object but the psychological subject of the sentence.

267. *shu* 孰 is used in a slightly different way from previously (cf. note 181), here being 'who among?' rather than 'which of (two)?' It occurs again at 112b without any noun preceding it, simply meaning 'who?'

268. Another instance of the grammatical use of *chiao* 交 described in note 14.

269. This is a case of *chin* 今 'now' being used to introduce a conditional clause—'if now', 'supposing'. The *fu* 夫 after it is used as described in note 259.

270. Notice the use of *chih yü chin* 至於今 'coming to the present', a neat way of indicating a shift in the time of the action.

271.   The use of *fou* 否 here shows that *shan* 善 is conceived as verbal and therefore to be negatived by *pu* 不 and *fou* 否 rather than by *fei* 非.

272.   The word *wu* 勿, which normally functions as a negative imperative adverb, is occasionally used after a verb as here—'wishes *not* to pity him'.

273.   *ch'i k'o hu* 其可乎 provides us with another example of *ch'i* 其 used as an auxiliary verb, the clause meaning 'will it be all right?'

274.   *ch'i ho chi* 其何及 means 'what will it come to?' Notice that the auxiliary *ch'i* 其 is here separated from its verb *chi* 及 'to reach'.

275.   *jo ho erh k'o* 若何而可 means 'in such circumstances what may be done?'. There are several variants of this formula. Mencius sometimes has *ju chih ho tse k'o* 如之何則可.

276.   Notice how the position of *lao* 老 preceding *erh* 而 shows that it must be verbal—'being old'.

277.   The fact that the text has *hsing ch'i yü* 行其欲 followed immediately by *te ch'i so so* 得其所索, with the *yü* 欲 functioning as a noun and *so* 索 as a verb, breaking the parallelism, must indicate that *so* 索 was not readily usable as a noun in the sense here required.

278.   This is a usage of *nai* 乃 which we have not yet encountered: it means 'thus' and it has been suggested that it may be a phonetic fusion of *ju chih* 如之 (but cf. note 217).

279.   *chün ch'i t'u chih* 君其圖之 is a common formula in *Kuo-yü* and *Tso-chuan*. It means 'Your Lordship should ponder on this'. The *ch'i* 其 is here clearly not acting as a future indicative, but is a closely related imperative usage—'Your Lordship *will* (or "is to" or "should") ponder on this'.

280.   *tzu* 自 we have only met previously as a pronominal adverb, but here it is a preposition meaning 'from'. *tzu . . . i lai* 自 . . . 以來 'from . . . onwards' is a fairly common idiom which should be noted. A similar idiom is *tzu chin i wang* 自今以往 'henceforward', and one also meets *tzu . . . i shang* 自 . . . 以上 and *tzu . . . i hsia* 自 . . . 以下 meaning 'from . . . upwards' and 'from . . . downwards', e.g. *tzu wang i hsia* 自王以下 'from the king downwards'. In general *tzu* 自 operates in the same way as *yu* 由 (see note 115).

281.   *yü* 與 is here the verb 'to give'—'he cannot be given the government'.

282.   Notice that in a statement replying to the *chün ch'i t'u chih* 君其圖之 he reverts to the normal *chiang* 將. The *ch'i* 其 certainly seems to be more common in questions and commands, and I am doubtful whether it ever occurs in the first person indicative.

283.   Here is a case of *i* 以 introducing a causal clause followed in the next line with *i* 以 introducing a purpose clause. The formal difference between the two is that the former has a subject, but the latter has not.

284.   *yu* 又 is a coordinate conjunction linking clauses, meaning 'also', 'furthermore'. Notice also the construction of this clause. We have to say 'fear

that borderlands will be annexed' or 'fear the annexation of borderlands', but the Chinese merely retains the verb-object pattern ('annex-borderlands') and makes it the object of the verb 'to fear', without implying that the subject of both verbs is the same. Similarly *k'ung ai jen* 恐愛人 means 'fear love-of-others', not necessarily 'fear to love others'.

285.　　This usage of *kuo* 果 is akin to the sense 'really', 'actually' that we have met before (see note 127). Here it is functioning as a noun and the whole phrase means *'the reality (or truth)* of his situation vis-à-vis the masses'.

286.　　*k'o* 可 on its own means '(it) is all right', '(it) is O.K.'.

287.　　For this use of *i* 益 see note 188.

288.　　For this use of *nai* 乃 see note 278.

289.　　*ch'ieh fu* 且夫 is found in some writers, including all those represented in this book, with the same meaning as *ch'ieh* 且 'moreover', q.v. note 218.

290.　　This is an instance of a special use of *ssu* 四, 'four', meaning 'on all four sides'. The expression *ssu i* 四夷 'the barbarians on all four sides' and *ssu hai* 四海 'the seas on all four sides' also occur commonly.

291.　　Notice the useful part played by the *ch'i* 其 here: the sentence, which must be rendered in English by 'the advantages of knowing whether it is possible or not are numerous', splits neatly into two short clauses. The function of the *ch'i* 其 at 123t is similar.

292.　　Here, with the duke's reaction to Li Chi's speech, we have a typical situation in which 說 must be taken as standing for *yüeh* 悅; cf. the passage discussed in note 193.

PASSAGE J

CH'UNG-ERH, another son of Duke Hsien of Chin, has returned after a long exile and become ruler of Chin. He is rewarding his loyal supporters. Hui and Huai (126c, d) are the posthumous names of two other sons of Duke Hsien who had already occupied the Chin throne (from *Tso-chuan*, Duke Hsi section, year 24).

293.　　The Marquis of Chin is Ch'ung-erh, son of Duke Hsien of Chin. Hsien-kung, Duke Hsien (125 s–t), is the posthumous title of a former ruler, all rulers of the feudal states being given the title of *kung* after their deaths. But Chin is a marquisate, so living rulers are called Marquises of Chin.

294.　　When groups of people are enumerated, the pattern noun-number-*jen*, as here, is common: instead of 'Duke Hsien had nine sons' we have 'Duke Hsien's sons (were) nine persons' (cf. note 202).

295.　　*tsai* 在 means 'to be in', 'to be present', and this is a case where the force of the *i* 矣 can perhaps best be rendered by the use of a different verb with a more active, less stative connotation, e.g. 'only His Highness *has survived*', rather than 'only His Highness is here now'.

296.   This is a good example of the kind of situation in which an active verb is better translated into a passive verb in English. 'They were rejected both at home and abroad' is the natural English equivalent of the Chinese clause.

297.   This is a good illustration of the functional flexibility of Chinese words. *chu* 主 appears first as a noun and immediately afterwards as a transitive verb. The meaning content is the same, but in English we have to reflect the difference of function by translating one as 'presider', 'president', and the other as 'presides'.

298.   Here we encounter another interrogative pronoun, *shui* 誰 meaning 'who?' Notice the combination with *fei* 非 'who if not?', 'who but?', reminiscent of the construction with *fei* 非 and *pu* 不 'if not . . . not', 'nothing but', referred to in note 153. Note that the *shui* 誰 can stand on its own after the *erh* 而, just as we can say 'if not then who?', the 'who?' forming a clause with verb understood.

299.   The function of *shih* 實 in *Tso-chuan* is that of a demonstrative related to *shih* 是 and placing emphasis on the subject of a sentence, i.e. 'Heaven—this—established him'. The effect has to be achieved in English by a circumlocution such as 'it was *heaven* that established him'. The usual meaning of *shih* 實 in other texts is 'real', 'really', 'sincere', 'solid', 'full'. For the comparable use of *shih* 是 to place emphasis on the object, see note 266.

300.   *erh san tzu* 二三子 'two or three gentlemen' is used several times in the *Analects* as Confucius's mode of address to a group of his disciples, but here and elsewhere in the *Tso-chuan* it is used in the third person. Notice that *erh san* 二三 means 'two *or* three'. Only if numbers appear in sequence can they be interpreted thus.

301.   A *chih* 之 can be understood between the *i* 以 and the *wei* 為 (cf. note 114).

302.   The use of *chi* 己 'self' invites comparison with that of *tzu* 自 (see note 158). The explanation of the difference between them lies in the position they occupy in relation to the verb, *tzu* 自 preceding the verb in the adverbial position and *chi* 己 following it as object in sentences of very similar meaning. Thus *tzu pi* 自比 is a simple reflexive—'he compared himself' (the *tzu* 自 functioning as a pronominal adverb qualifying the verb), but *cheng chi* 正己 'he corrected himself' lays much more emphasis on the physical person—'he adjusted his stance' (as, e.g., in *Mencius* IIa. 7). Since *tzu* 自 is adverbial and *chi* 己 nominal, only the latter can appear after prepositions. *chi* 己 is also found as or in apposition to the subject of a sentence ('he *himself* did it'), and *tzu* 自 also occurs adverbially but without being reflexive ('he *personally* did it'). The compound *tzu chi* 自己 also occurs as subject. In indirect speech in a sentence like 'the people thought that he would rescue themselves' the 'themselves' is rendered by *chi* 己 because it is not reflexive (see *Mencius* Ib. 11). In the present context we have *chi* 己 in possessive relationship with the following noun—'their own power', the possessive *chih* 之 being, as often, omitted.

303.   *yu* 猶 is a common grammatical word. It has two closely related mean-ings: (1) as a conjunction meaning 'nevertheless', as here; (2) as an adverb meaning 'still', e.g. *t'ien-hsia yu wei p'ing* 天下猶未平, 'the world was still unsettled' (*Mencius* IIIa. 4). *yu* 猶 can also mean 'like', but, as compared with *ju* 如 and *jo* 若, it comes in non-verbal sentences, i.e. X *yu* Y *yeh* X 猶 Y 也 means 'X is like Y'.

304.   The English for this is 'is called robbery': we use the passive construc-tion, but the Chinese idiom is 'call it robbery' with subject unexpressed.

305.   *hsiang* 相 means 'mutually', 'each other' and, like *chiao* 交 which has the same meaning, it appears in the adverbial position, immediately before the verb. It has related non-grammatical usages: as an adverb—'in co-operation', 'together'; as a verb—'to assist'; and as a noun—'a minister'. It is often used in contrast with the reflexive *tzu* 自 (see note 158). Occasionally it is used loosely in the sense of 'anyone else', e.g. *mo neng hsiang shang* 莫能相尚, 'nobody can excel anybody else' (*Mencius* IIb. 2); or 'others of their own kind', e.g. *shou hsiang shih* 獸相食 'animals eat their own kind' (*Mencius*, Ia. 4).

306.   Just as *chih* 之 is always omitted after the prepositional *i* 以, similarly it is sometimes omitted after the prepositional *yü* 與.

307.   Some texts punctuate before this *i ssu* 以死 rather than after it, but the expression occurs elsewhere in *Tso-chuan* at the end of a sentence with the meaning 'until death', which fits the context here. The use of *i* 以 is unusual, but somewhat reminiscent of its occurrence in the phrases mentioned in note 280.

308.   In addition to its usage as a coordinate conjunction meaning 'also', 'further', 'in addition', *yu* 又 serves to intensify a comparative, as here. *yu shen yen* 又甚焉 means 'even worse than it'.

309.   Another case where the Chinese active verb would more naturally be put into the passive in English since it has no definite subject. We would say 'cause it to be known about', 'make it known'.

310.   *jo ho* 若何 and *jo chih ho* 若之何 occur commonly in *Tso-chuan* meaning '(in a situation) like this, what about . . .?' Mencius never has either of these expressions, only the rather similar *ju chih ho* 如之何 (see note 138), but this is always followed by a clause, while *jo ho* 若何 and *jo chih ho* 若之何 often conclude a sentence.

311.   For *yen yung* 焉用 'what is the use of?' cf. note 160.

312.   This is a clear example of *ju* 如 in the sense of 'to do like', rather than the more usual 'to be like'.

313.   The second person pronoun *ju* 汝 is often written like this without the water radical, as if it were *nü*, 'woman'.

314.   Notice the use of *chieh* 偕 here. It is obviously related to *chieh* 皆 'all', 'both', which we have already had, but it is often used in combination with

73

yü 與 to form 'together with', the *yü* 與 preceding the noun and the *chieh* 偕 succeeding it.

315.   *sui* 遂 'then', 'next', 'accordingly' is a common link-word between episodes in narrative passages.

316.   This sentence illustrates the undesirability of always translating *erh* 而 as if it were 'and' or 'but' and thus failing to give proper weight to the second clause. Thus, instead of 'accordingly they went into retirement and died' one should translate 'accordingly they died in retirement'. It fits the context much better to take what happened 'accordingly' as one thing, viz. death-in-retirement, rather than two, retirement and then death.

Notice also that there is only one word between *erh* 而 and the pause indicated by a full-stop. By using the concordances published in the Harvard-Yenching Sinological Index Series it is easy to draw up a list of words which are found between *erh* 而 and pause and discover a word-class with this feature in common. Similarly we can discover a word-class consisting of words which appear between *pu* 不 and pause. On investigation these will all be found to be words which we already know be translatable as verbs. In other words a verb in Chinese may be defined as a word which can occur between *erh* 而 and pause or between *pu* 不 and pause. Similarly a noun may be defined as a word which can occur between the words *wu* 無 or *yü* 於 and pause. The two classes are not, of course, mutually exclusive.

Other evidence may be used to establish the nominal character of a word, e.g. if a word can be preceded by a number, it must be a noun. Thus, although a word's class-membership is not so obvious and clear-cut in Chinese as it is in inflected languages, there is no doubt that a system of word-classes exists.

317.   Notice the double object after *wei* 為, following exactly the same pattern as the English 'made him a field', with nothing to distinguish the indirect object from the direct object except that the indirect object comes first.

318.   Here we have a usage of *ch'ieh* 且 which is slightly different from that described in note 218. Instead of being a conjunction between entirely unrelated sentences ('moreover'), it here links two parallel purpose clauses introduced by *i* 以 and must be translated 'and'.

PASSAGE K

A grandee from the state of Cheng in central China uses subtle argument on the Earl of the powerful western state of Ch'in to ward off attack and secure a treaty with Ch'in (from *Tso-chuan*, Duke Hsi section, year 30).

319.   Dates are given in the order 'year, month, day', with the name of the day being given in terms of a hexagenary cycle, details of which can be found in dictionaries and reference works. Note that there is no distinction between cardinal and ordinal numbers: *chiu* 九 means both 'nine' and 'ninth'. Notice

also that no prepositions are needed when dates and times are given. Other examples occur later in this passage: 'at night' (136y), 'in the morning' (140i), 'in the evening' (140l).

320. Here *i* 以 introduces a causal clause which is terminated by *yeh* 也, as often when it succeeds the main clause and gives an explanation for an action which has been narrated. The *ch'ieh* 且 again links the two *i*-clauses (cf. note 318).

321. The verb *chün* 軍 'encamp' is generally followed by *yü* 於 'at', but the preposition is omitted here.

322. *jo shih* 若使 is sometimes used to introduce a hypothesis—'if you cause it to be that', 'supposing', but here the lack of another verb to serve as the main verb of the clause shows that *shih* 使 is being used in a non-grammatical sense, i.e. 'to send'.

323. This noun—*chih* 之—verb—*yeh* 也 pattern is often found in the *Tso-chuan* where we would use a temporal clause—'when I was able-bodied'. For the quasi-pronominal use of *ch'en* 臣 see note 72.

324. This is *yu* 猶 meaning 'still', 'nevertheless' (see note 303). A more natural translation may often be obtained by using the word 'even' with the preceding clause—'even when I was able-bodied'.

325. Notice that *jen* 人 sometimes means 'other men', 'others'. For another pronominal use of *jen* 人 see note 139.

326. Notice again the force of the *i* 矣 in 'now I *have become* old', as contrasted with the *yeh* 也 in 'when I was young'. It not only makes it clear that *lao* 老 is verbal, but also indicates that the action of the verb is completed.

327. Notice that it is possible to have *wu neng* 無能 followed by a verb as well as *pu neng* 不能. In the latter case *neng* 能 functions as an auxiliary verb, and in the former as a noun, object of *wu* 無—'I lack the *ability*'.

328. In *yeh i* 也已 we have a formation which is rare and therefore difficult to interpret, but an inspection of the occurrences in the *Tso-chuan* suggests that it might serve as a combination of *yeh* 也 and *erh i* 而已, viz. to describe a continuing state emphatically and with finality—'I definitely lack the ability to take action'.

329. From *wu* 吾 to *tzu* 子 looks like a verbal sentence, but in fact *wu* 吾 must be taken as possessive, forming a long substantival clause ('the fact that I . . .'); the whole being resumed by the demonstrative pronoun *shih* 是.

330. Notice here the use of *pu* 不 as a privative with a noun, *pu li* 不利 meaning 'disadvantage'.

331. Earlier we noticed that *chih* 知 could be followed directly by a verb in the sense of 'to know that one should do something' (see note 60). Here we have *chih wang* 知亡 (rather than *chih ch'i wang* 知其亡) for 'to know that *it* is ruined'.

332. Often in the *Tso-chuan* one meets *kan* 敢 in a sentence which looks indicative but which does not make sense unless one supplies an interrogative final particle *hu* 乎. 'Would I dare to . . .?' is the translation in the present context. Later writers, when using material which has appeared in the *Tso-chuan*, supply this *hu* 乎 in such contexts. *kan* 敢 is sometimes followed by *i* 以 'therefore', as here.

333. Notice that *chih-shih* 執事 is a verb-object compound noun formed on the same pattern as *yu-ssu* 有司 (see note 108).

334. *pi* 鄙 is here verbal—'to make a dependency of'. This sentence is a typical example of the abrupt *Tso* style. *yüan* 遠 is used by itself for 'remote countries', 'remote place', and there is no adjective with *kuo* 國 to suggest '*intervening* countries'. Another frequent difficulty, which presents itself here too, is that of determining the subject. Here the answer is that the verbs have no subject. The clause *yüeh kuo i pi yüan* 越國以鄙遠 is a substantival clause which fits into the pattern of the sentence through the device of being resumed by the possessive pronoun *ch'i* 其—'you understand the difficulty of going beyond intervening countries to make a dependency of a remote place'.

335. The *so* 所 here should be taken as if it were *so yü* 所於 (which, as pointed out in note 198, does not exist), i.e. 'you will therefore not have that in respect of which you are harmed' or 'there will be no respect in which you suffer harm'. The *so* 所 cannot be taken as the object of *hai* 害 since this verb means 'to harm', not 'to suffer harm' or 'to be harmed', which is the meaning required by the context. It must therefore be taken as passive.

336. Notice that where we would say '*as* you know' the Chinese uses *so* 所—'that which you know'. This is the regular idiom.

337. For *ho yen chih yu* 何厭之有 cf. note 197.

338. This use of *yu* 又 is different from the coordinate conjunction loosely linking two clauses ('moreover', 'furthermore'). It is an adverbial 'also', rather like *i* 亦. The essential difference between the two examples is that here the subject of the clause succeeding the *yu* 又 is the same as that of the clause preceding the *yu* 又, but in the example discussed in note 284 there is a change of subject.

339. As explained in note 131, the interrogative adverb *yen* 焉 is equivalent to *yü* 於 + an interrogative pronoun. Since *yü* 於 can mean 'from', *yen* 焉 can mean 'whence', and that is the sense of it here.

340. The use of *wei* 唯 'only' with this expression, which we have met before (see note 279), may be rendered idiomatically by 'it is up to you alone to'.

APPENDIX A

GRAMMATICAL USAGES WHICH DO NOT OCCUR IN THE TEXT-PASSAGES

IN ORDER to make this book more comprehensive I provide here some explanation of usages which are not encountered in the text-passages. Some of these usages involve words which have already occurred in other senses, but others involve words which do not occur in these text-passages at all. I have omitted very rare grammatical words and only included ones which the student can reasonably be expected to become familiar with. The characters are given in radical and stroke order, and the figure on the left of each character indicates the number of the radical and the number of additional strokes. References to *Chuang-tzu* and *Mo-tzu* are to the texts printed with the Harvard-Yenching concordances of those works, references to the *Analects* and *Mencius* are to chapter and verse, and references to the *Tso-chuan* are to page and column in Legge's edition. For abbreviations see the introduction to the vocabulary (page 89).

1/4   且   **ch'ieh³** · *aux. v.* be about to, shall: e.g. 病愈我且往見 (*Mencius* IIIa.5) 'When I am better, I shall go and see him'.

1/8   並   **ping⁴** *adv.* together: e.g. (a) 亂虐並生 (*Tso-chuan* 456.12) 'Disorders and oppressions grow up together'; e.g. (b) (in the pattern 與 X 並, 'together with X') 賢者與民並耕 (*Mencius* IIIa.4) 'The able and virtuous plough together with the people'.

7/1   于   **yü²** *prep.* used like 於.

9/5   余   **yü²** *personal pron.* used like 予.

9/8   俱   **chü⁴** *adv.* together: e.g. (a) 莫不俱至 (*Chuang-tzu* 12/73) 'All arrive together'; e.g. (b) (in the pattern 與 X 俱, 'together with X') 雖與之俱學 (*Mencius* VIa.9) 'Although he is learning together with him'; *pron.* both: e.g. 其俱是也 (*Chuang-tzu* 2/86) 'Both of us are right'.

12/6   其   **ch'i²** *adj.* such, so much. It must be remembered that 其 stands for noun + 之. This is easy enough when the 之 is possessive, but more puzzling when 其 stands for noun + determinative 之 其國, if it refers back to 齊王之國, means 'his state', but if it referred back to 萬乘之國 it would mean 'such a state': e.g. 齊有其地 (*Mencius* IIa.1) 'Ch'i had so much territory' (其地 stands for 千里之地).

18/5   初   **ch'u¹** *adv.* for the first time: e.g. 齊子初聘於齊 (*Tso-chuan* 485.11) 'Ch'i-tzu for the first time went on a mission to Ch'i'; before this (used in the *Tso-chuan* to introduce 'flashbacks', i.e. incidents in the *Tso-chuan* which took place some time earlier than the year under which they are entered).

29/2   及   **chi²** *conj.* (linking nouns) and, together with; *conj.* (linking clauses) when: e.g 及陷乎罪 (*Mencius* IIIa.3) 'When they are involved in crime'; *prep.* by, until, up to: e.g. 及寡人之身 (*Mencius* Ia.5) 'By my lifetime'.

30/3   各   **ko⁴** *adv.* each: e.g. 人各有能有不能 (*Tso-chuan* 356.2) 'Men each have their abilities and disabilities'; *pron.* each: e.g. 各欲正己 (*Mencius* VIIb.4) 'Each wished to correct itself'.

31/3 因 **yin¹** *v.t.* take advantage of, rely on; *verb-prep.* relying on, because of, through the agency of, by the help of; *conj.* therefore: e.g. 無恆產因無恆心 (*Mencius* Ia.7) 'They lack a constant livelihood and therefore they lack a constant mind'.

37/1 夫 **fu²** *interrog. final particle* used for 否乎: e.g. 吾死矣夫 (*Mencius* IVb.24) 'I shall die, shall I not?'

40/3 安 **an¹** *adj.* quiet, peaceful; *v.t.* pacify; *adv.* how?, where?, in what respect?, whence?, for what? (used in the same way as 焉 and probably related to it): e.g. 立而不從, 將安用君 (*Tso-chuan* 407.3) 'If after installing him they do not support him, what use will they have for a ruler?' (literally 'for what will they use a ruler?').

42/5 尚 **shang⁴** *adv., conj.* still, nevertheless: e.g. 今吾尚病 (*Mencius* IIIa.5) 'Now I am still ill'.

52/9 幾 **chi³** *interrog. adj.* how many?: e.g. 不知其幾千里 (*Chuang-tzu* 1/1) 'I do not know how many thousand *li* it is';
chi¹ *adv.* almost: e.g. 不從晉, 國幾亡 (*Tso-chuan* 450.4) 'Through our not following Chin the state is nearly ruined'; used in 庶幾 shu⁴ chi¹, *adv.* perhaps, probably.

60/7 徒 **t'u²** *adv.* only (used also in 非徒 fei¹ t'u², not only; used in 豈徒 ch'i³ t'u², surely not only): e.g. 非徒無益而又害之 (*Mencius* IIa.2) 'It is not only of no benefit, but also harms it'; *adj.* sole, alone: e.g. 徒善不足以為政 (*Mencius* IVa.1) 'Goodness alone is not adequate for the exercise of government'.

60/9 徧 **pien⁴** *adv.* universally, everywhere (N.B. often although it qualifies the verb it relates to the object, as in the following example): e.g. 不徧愛人 (*Mencius* VIIa.46) 'did not love all men' (literally 'did not universally love men').

60/10 微 **wei¹** *adj.* small, minute; *prep.* but for: e.g. 微子則不及此 (*Tso-chuan* 155.5) 'But for you I would not have reached this position'.

66/8 敝 **pi⁴** *adj.* worn-out, poor, worthless; *quasi-pron.* (derived from the preceding meaning) my/our unworthy, my/our: e.g. 敝邑 (*Tso-chuan* passim) 'our city'.

70/0 方 **fang¹** *conj.* while, so long as, at the moment when: e.g. 方其夢也 不知其夢也 (*Chuang-tzu* 2/81) 'While they dream, they do not know that they dream'.

80/3 每 **mei³** *adj.* each, every: e.g. 每人 (*Mencius* IVb.2) 'each man'; *conj.* each time, whenever: e.g. 每朝, 其妻必戒之 (*Tso-chuan* 387.16) 'Each time he attended court, his wife always warned him'.

94/9 猶 **yu²** *copula* is like: e.g. 牛之性猶人之性與 (*Mencius* VIa.3) 'Is the nature of an ox like the nature of a man?'

102/6 畢 **pi⁴** *adv.* all: e.g. 師畢入 (*Tso-chuan* 797.17) 'When his troops had all entered'.

102/8 當 **tang¹** *prep.* at, during: e.g. 當是時 (passim) 'at this time'.

108/9 盡 **chin⁴** *adv.* entirely, fully, utterly (N.B. although it qualifies the verb, it generally relates to the object, as in the following example): e.g. 盡出之 (*Tso-chuan* 438.17) 'They brought forth all of them'.

120/11 縱 **tsung⁴** *v.t.* allow; *conj.* granted that, even if, although: e.g. 縱無法以遺後嗣 (*Tso-chuan* 242.11) 'Granted that he had no example to leave to posterity'.

123/7 羣 **ch'ün²** *n.* flock, group, crowd; *adj.* all (generally used like 諸 to qualify groups of people): e.g. 羣公子 'all the princes', 羣臣 'all the ministers'.

126/0 而 **erh²** The following are the main exceptions to the rule that 而 is a conjunction which subordinates the clause which precedes it to the one which follows it: (i) when the clause preceding the 而 is the main clause and the clause following it is a purpose or consequence clause: e.g. (a) 率天下之人而禍仁義者, 必子之言夫

(*Mencius* VIa.1) 'What leads all men on to consider humanity and justice as calamities must be your words, must it not?'; e.g. (b) 有一言而可以終身用之者乎 (*Analects* XV.23) 'Is there a single saying such that one can act upon it throughout one's life?';

(ii) when 而 is preceded by an expression of place or time: e.g. (a) 欲中國而授孟子室 (*Mencius* IIb.10) 'I wish to give Mencius a house at the capital'; e.g. (b) 三日而死 (*Chuang-tzu* 18/35) 'On the third day it died' (in such examples the 而 makes no difference to the meaning, but by imposing a break between the expression preceding the 而 and the verb it places a slight emphasis on that expression);

(iii) when 而 comes between subject and verb, it serves to emphasize the subject: e.g. 管氏而知禮, 孰不知禮 (*Analects* III.22) 'If *even* Kuan Chung understands the rites, who does not understand the rites?'

130/5 胡 **hu**[2] *interrog. adv.* how?, why?: e.g. 胡可比也 (*Tso-chuan* 64.7) 'How can they be compared?'

134/10 舉 **chü**[3] *v.t.* lift, promote; *adj.* all, the whole (sometimes succeeds the noun as in 君舉不信羣臣乎 [*Tso-chuan* 475.21] 'Do rulers all distrust all their ministers?').

147/0 見 **chien**[4] *aux. v.* which, preceding another verb, puts that verb into the passive: e.g. 愛人者必見愛也 (*Mo-tzu* 16/71) 'He who loves others is bound to be loved'.

APPENDIX B

TRANSLATION OF PASSAGES A–E

PASSAGE A

Mencius saw King Hui of Liang. 'Venerable sir,' he said, 'since you have come here, not thinking a thousand leagues too long a journey, you will therefore possess the means to profit my kingdom, will you not?'

'Why must Your Majesty mention profit?' replied Mencius. 'What I "therefore" have with me is humanity and justice and nothing more. If Your Majesty says "How may I profit my state?", the grandees will say "How may we profit our houses?", and the knights and the common people will say "How may we profit ourselves?"; and if superiors and inferiors contend with each other for profit, the state will be endangered. He who assassinates the sovereign of a ten-thousand-chariot state will become the head of a thousand-chariot house, and he who assassinates the sovereign of a thousand-chariot state will become the head of a hundred-chariot house. To gain a thousand out of ten-thousand or to gain a hundred out of a thousand would not seem a small reward; so if you are reputed to put justice last and profit first, your people will never be satisfied unless they are helping themselves. It never happens that one who is humane abandons his parents or that one who is just repudiates his sovereign. Let Your Majesty therefore talk only of humanity and justice. What need is there to mention profit?'

PASSAGE B

'As for my attitude towards the state,' said King Hui of Liang, 'I do indeed devote my whole attention to it. When there is a disaster in Honei I move some of its people from there to Hotung and move some of Hotung's grain to Honei. When there is a disaster in Hotung I also employ a similar remedy. An investigation of the government of neighbouring states will show that such devotion as I display is absent. Why is it, then, that the people of neighbouring states do not decrease and my people do not increase?'

'Your Majesty is fond of war,' replied Mencius, 'so I beg to explain this by means of a military illustration. The drums are rumbling to sound the advance, but as soon as the blades have clashed the soldiers flee, abandoning their armour and trailing their weapons behind them. Some run a hundred paces before stopping and others run fifty paces before stopping. What if the latter ridiculed a hundred paces on the strength of their fifty paces?'

'That would be wrong,' said the king. 'The only difference was simply that they did not go a hundred paces, but their behaviour was just as much a case of running away.'

'If Your Majesty were to understand this,' said Mencius, 'then you would not expect your people to become more numerous than the inhabitants of neighbouring states. If the farming seasons are not disregarded, there will be more than enough grain to eat; if nets with too fine a mesh are not put into the fishponds, there will be more than enough fish and turtles to eat; if axes are taken into the upland forests only in due season, there will be more than enough timber to use. If there is more than enough grain and fish and turtles to eat and more than enough timber to use, this will ensure that the people, both in their care of the living and in their mourning for the dead, will be without bitterness. When they are without bitterness both in their care of the living and in their mourning for the dead, it is the beginning of princely government. Plant five-acre homesteads with mulberry trees, and those who are fifty may wear silk. Do not neglect the due seasons for the breeding of fowls, pigs, and dogs, and those who are seventy may eat meat. Do not deprive the hundred-acre estates of labour in due season, and the households with many mouths to feed may escape hunger. Pay careful heed to education in the schools, giving increased attention to the duties of filial piety and fraternal respect, and those who are grey-haired will not be carrying burdens upon the highways. If those who are seventy wear silk and eat meat and the ordinary people suffer neither hunger nor cold, the ruler who has brought such things to pass is bound to become a true king. Although dogs and pigs eat food fit for human beings, you do not understand that you should introduce regulations* against this; while at the same time there are people dying of starvation upon the roads, but you do not understand that you should dole out grain to them. When people die you say: "It is not my fault; it is the harvest." How does this differ from killing a man by stabbing him and then saying: "It was not me; it was the weapon"? Do not put the blame on the harvests, Your Majesty, and then peoples from throughout the world will come to you.'

PASSAGE C

'May I be told about the deeds of Huan of Ch'i and Wen of Chin?' enquired King Hsüan of Ch'i.

'Among the followers of Confucius there was no one who talked about the deeds of Huan and Wen,' replied Mencius, 'and consequently later generations have had nothing handed down to them, and I myself have learned nothing of these matters. Since I am not equipped to deal with them, what about true kingship?'

'With what sort of virtue may one become king?', he said.

'One may become king by protecting the people—nobody could prevent it,' said Mencius.

* A well attested alternative reading here is *lien* 歛 instead of *chien* 捡. If this reading were adopted the translation would be: 'You do not understand that you should store it up'. I prefer to retain the text as it stands since it is clear from *Mencius* Ia.4 that Mencius is not complaining against a failure to store up food for the lean years, but is attacking a state of affairs in which animals are being well fed *at the same time as* human beings are starving.

'Could someone like me really protect the people?'

'Yes.'

'How do you know that I could?'

'I was told the following story by Hu Ho: Your Majesty was sitting at the top of the hall when someone went past the bottom of the hall leading an ox. "Where is the ox going?" you said when you saw it, and the reply was: "We are about to consecrate a bell with its blood." "Release it!" you said, "for I will not endure its shuddering like an innocent approaching the place of execution." The reply was: "In that case shall we dispense with the consecration of the bell?" "How can it be dispensed with?" you said. "Replace it with a sheep." I don't know whether this really happened.'

'It did,' said the king.

'Such a heart is capable of exercising true kingship,' said Mencius. 'The common people all thought that Your Majesty was being parsimonious, but I fully understand that you would not endure it.'

'Yes,' said the king, 'there really are such people; but surely I wouldn't begrudge a single ox, even if the state of Ch'i were tiny. Just at that moment I could not put up with its shuddering like an innocent approaching the place of execution, and that is why I replaced it with a sheep.'

'Your Majesty should not see anything odd in the fact that the common people thought you were being parsimonious,' said Mencius. 'How else were they to understand your replacing the larger with the smaller? If Your Majesty felt pained at its approaching the place of death although innocent, what was there to choose between an ox and a sheep?'

'What really were my motives in this?' said the king with a smile. 'It is not that I replaced it with a sheep because I begrudged the expense of it. Yet there is justification for the common people saying that I did begrudge it.'

'There's no harm done,' said Mencius. 'This is just the way benevolence works. You saw the ox but never saw the sheep. Gentlemen are like this with animals—when they have seen them alive they will not endure to see them die, and when they have heard their cries they will not endure to eat their flesh. It is for this reason that the gentleman places his kitchen in the furthest part of the house.'

PASSAGE D

Duke P'ing of Lu was about to go out, when a certain Tsang Ts'ang who was one of his favourites made a request of him. 'When Your Highness has gone out on other occasions,' he said, 'you have always instructed your officials where you were going. This time the horses are already harnessed to your carriage, but your officials do not yet know where you are going. May I make so bold as to enquire?'

'I am going to visit Mencius,' said the duke.

'What!' he exclaimed. 'Is it because you think of him as a man of virtue that you demean yourself to pay the first call on a commoner? Propriety and righteousness spring from men of virtue; but the funeral Mencius provided for his mother was more lavish than the one he provided for his father who died earlier.* Do not go and see him, Your Highness.'

The duke agreed not to go, but when Yo-cheng Tzu came in and had audience of him he said: 'Why did Your Highness not visit Mencius?'

He replied: 'Someone told me that the second funeral Mencius provided was more lavish than the first, and that is why I did not go and visit him.'

'What is it that Your Highness means by "more lavish"?' he exclaimed. 'Is it that on the earlier occasion he acted in accordance with the ceremony appropriate to a knight, while on the later occasion he acted in accordance with the ceremony appropriate to a grandee? Is it that on the earlier occasion he used three cauldrons, but on the later occasion five?'

'No,' he said. 'What I am referring to is the quality of the coffin and of the burial clothing.'

'But that is not what one means by being more lavish,' he said. 'It is a question of the difference in his financial situation.'

Yo-cheng Tzu went to see Mencius. 'I made representations to His Highness,' he said, 'and he was intending to come and see you. But one of his favourites, a certain Tsang Ts'ang, stopped him, and that is why he did not actually come.'

'If a man makes progress,' said Mencius, 'he may have been helped on his way, and if he stops he may have been hindered; but the progress and the stopping are not within another man's power to bring about. The fact that I did not meet the prince of Lu was decreed by Heaven. How could a mere member of the Tsang family have prevented me from meeting him?'

PASSAGE E

Mencius was about to attend the king's court when a messenger arrived from His Majesty. 'I was practically on my way to visit you,' ran the king's message, 'but I have a cold and I ought not to expose myself to this wind. However, if you will come to court, I will myself attend there. I do not know whether I may be granted an opportunity of seeing you there?'

'Unfortunately I am unwell,' replied Mencius, 'and cannot go to court.'

On the following day he went out to convey his condolences to the Tung-kuo family on a recent bereavement. 'Yesterday,' said Kung-sun Ch'ou, 'you excused yourself on account of illness, but today you pay a visit of condolence. Might I suggest that this is improper?'

'Yesterday I was ill, but today I am better,' said Mencius, 'so in these circumstances why should I not pay a vist of condolence?'

The king sent someone to enquire after his health, and a physician also arrived. Meng Chung-tzu replied to the messenger. 'Yesterday,' he said, 'when he received the king's command, he was suffering from a trifling indisposition, and was unable to go to court. Today he felt somewhat better and hastened off to court. I do not know whether he can have got there or not?' He then sent

* Literally 'his later mourning exceeded his earlier mourning.'

several people off to intercept Mencius on the road and say: 'Please, whatever you do, don't come home, but instead go along to the court!'

Mencius felt that he had no alternative but to go to Ching Ch'ou's place and stay the night there. Ching Ch'ou said to him: 'In private the tie which binds father and son and in public the link between ruler and minister—these are the most important of human relationships. The father-son relationship places the greatest emphasis on love, and the ruler-minister relationship places the greatest emphasis on respect. I notice that the king treats you with respect, but I have never observed how you show your respect for the king.'

'Oh! What a thing to say!' exclaimed Mencius. 'There is no-one among the men of Ch'i who converses with His Majesty about benevolence and righteousness, and this is surely not because they consider benevolence and righteousness to be undesirable. If they simply think: "This fellow is not worth conversing with about benevolence and righteousness", that shows the greatest possible disrespect. For my part I would not venture to set before the king anything but the principles of Yao and Shun, and so nobody among the men of Ch'i shows such respect for the king as I do.'

THE 214 RADICALS
with their Abbreviated and Alternative Forms

The type used throughout this book has been chosen because it looks like handwriting and is therefore suitable for the student to copy, but for the sake of comparison the normal printed form of the radicals is also included in this list.

1 stroke

1	一	一
2	丨	丨
3	丶	丶
4	丿	丿
5	乙	乙
6	亅	亅

2 strokes

7	二	二
8	亠	亠
9	人, 亻	人, 亻
10	儿	儿
11	入	入
12	八	八
13	冂	冂
14	冖	冖
15	冫	冫
16	几	几
17	凵	凵
18	刀 刂	刀 刂
19	力	力
20	勹	勹
21	匕	匕
22	匚	匚
23	匸	匸
24	十	十
25	卜	卜
26	卩, 巳	卩, 巳
27	厂	厂
28	厶	厶
29	又	又

阝 see 163, 170 阝

3 strokes

30	口	口
31	囗	囗
32	土	土
33	士	士
34	夂	夂
35	夊	夊
36	夕	夕
37	大	大
38	女	女
39	子	子
40	宀	宀
41	寸	寸
42	小	小
43	尢	尢
44	尸	尸
45	屮	屮
46	山	山
47	巛 川	巛, 川
48	工	工
49	己	己
50	巾	巾
51	干	干

#	Radical	Variant	#	Radical	Variant	#	Radical	Variant
52	幺	幺	70	方	方	94	犬, 犭	犬, 犭
53	广	广	71	无, 旡	无, 旡		王 see 96	王
54	廴	廴	72	日	日		耂 see 125	耂
55	廾	廾	73	曰	曰		辶 see 162	辶
56	弋	弋	74	月 (cf. 130)	月		礻 see 113	礻
57	弓	弓	75	木	木		艹 see 140	艹
58	彐, 彑	彐, 彑	76	欠	欠			
59	彡	彡	77	止	止		**5 strokes**	
60	彳	彳	78	歹	歹			
	忄 see 61	忄	79	殳	殳	95	玄	玄
	扌 see 64	扌	80	母	母	96	玉, 王	玉, 王
	氵 see 85	氵	81	比	比	97	瓜	瓜
	犭 see 94	犭	82	毛	毛	98	瓦	瓦
			83	氏	氏	99	甘	甘
	4 strokes		84	气	气	100	生	生
			85	水, 氵	水, 氵	101	用	用
61	心, 忄, 小	心, 忄, 小	86	火, 灬	火, 灬	102	田	田
62	戈	戈	87	爪, 爫	爪, 爫	103	疋	疋
63	戶	戶	88	父	父	104	疒	疒
64	手, 扌	手, 扌	89	爻	爻	105	癶	癶
65	支	支	90	爿	爿	106	白	白
66	攴, 攵	攴, 攵	91	片	片	107	皮	皮
67	文	文	92	牙	牙	108	皿	皿
68	斗	斗	93	牛	牛	109	目, 罒 (cf. 122)	目, 罒
69	斤	斤				110	矛	矛

111	矢		矢		132	自		自
112	石		石		133	至		至
113	示	示	示	礻	134	白		白
114	卤		卤		135	舌		舌
115	禾		禾		136	舛		舛
116	穴		穴		137	舟		舟
117	立		立		138	艮		艮
	衤	see 145	衤		139	色		色

6 strokes

					140	艸	艹	艸	艹
118	竹	竹	竹	⺮	141	虍		虍
119	米		米		142	虫		虫
120	糸		糸		143	血		血
121	缶		缶		144	行		行
122	网	罒	网	罒	145	衣	衤	衣	衤
123	羊		羊		146	西		西
124	羽		羽					
125	老	耂	老	耂	**7 strokes**			
126	而		而		147	見		見
127	耒		耒		148	角		角
128	耳		耳		149	言	訁	言	訁
129	聿		聿		150	谷		谷
130	肉	月 (cf. 74)	肉	月	151	豆		豆
131	臣		臣		152	豕		豕
					153	豸		豸

154	貝		貝
155	赤		赤
156	走		走
157	足	⻊	足	⻊
158	身		身
159	車		車
160	辛		辛
161	辰		辰
162	辵	辶	辵	辶
163	邑	阝 (cf. 170)	邑	阝
164	酉		酉
165	釆		釆
166	里		里

8 strokes

167	金		金
168	長		長
169	門		門
170	阜	阝 (cf. 163)	阜	阝
171	隶		隶
172	隹		隹
173	雨		雨
174	青		青
175	非		非

9 strokes

176	面	面
177	革	革
178	韋	韋
179	韭	韭
180	音	音
181	頁	頁
182	風	風
183	飛	飛
184	食	食
185	首	首
186	香	香

10 strokes

| 187 | 馬 | 馬 |
| 188 | 骨 | 骨 |

189	高	高
190	髟	髟
191	鬥	鬥
192	鬯	鬯
193	鬲	鬲
194	鬼	鬼

11 strokes

195	魚	魚
196	鳥	鳥
197	鹵	鹵
198	鹿	鹿
199	麥	麥
200	麻	麻

12 strokes

| 201 | 黃 | 黃 |

202	黍	黍
203	黑	黑
204	黹	黹

13-17 strokes

205	黽	黽
206	鼎	鼎
207	鼓	鼓
208	鼠	鼠
209	鼻	鼻
210	齊	齊
211	齒	齒
212	龍	龍
213	龜	龜
214	龠	龠

VOCABULARY

THE following introductory notes should be read very carefully before the vocabulary is used:

1. No dictionary of Classical Chinese based on satisfactory lexicographical procedures was available as a guide in the compilation of this vocabulary. Research on the Classical Chinese language has mainly been concerned with the study of grammatical words, not with the behaviour and meaning of words in the general vocabulary of the language. This vocabulary therefore cannot be regarded as a piece of material based on exhaustive research, but it is hoped that it will be a useful tool to enable the beginner to dispense with dictionaries, which in the initial stages can be misleading as often as they are instructive.

2. I have assigned the various items in the vocabulary to word-classes for two reasons: a. There is, as I emphasize in note 316, a system of word-classes in the Chinese language, so an indication of the class to which the word always or normally belongs is bound to be helpful to the beginner; b. This procedure often makes the English definition clearer. For example, if we are told that 反 *fan* means 'return', we want to know whether it means 'go back', 'hand back', or 'homeward journey'. The addition of the abbreviations *v.i.*, *v.t.*, or *n.* will make this clear in the minimum of space.

At the same time it would be a waste of space to include all possible functions. Most nouns may be found functioning as adjectives, so I have not bothered to give their adjectival uses unless they are common (e.g. 中 *chung, adj.* central) or not immediately deducible from the substantival meaning (e.g. 世 *shih, adj.* hereditary).

It is also necessary to remind the reader of the danger of applying a system of word-classes too rigidly in a language of this kind, e.g. 必 *pi* may often be taken as either an auxiliary verb or an adverb (cf. note 18). Moreover even in English it is not always easy to decide whether a word is functioning as an adverb or a conjunction, so it would be absurd to expect to be able to make a foolproof distinction in Chinese.

3. I have omitted rare meanings and all meanings which do not occur in the five works used for this book and the literature contemporary with them.

4. Verbs are marked as intransitive if they never take an object with the meaning given, and transitive if they do sometimes take an object with the meaning given. If verbs marked as intransitive are encountered with an object, it will be found that they are being used in a causative or putative sense (cf. note 3). When such causative or putative usages are common, I have recorded them (e.g. 亂 *luan, v.i.* be in disorder; *v.t.* cause confusion in).

5.   No attempt is made in this vocabulary to summarize all the information given in this book about grammatical words, so definitions of these can only serve as a brief reminder of the information given in the notes and in the grammatical survey. References are given in brackets to places in the notes and grammatical survey where the essential information concerning the behaviour of a grammatical word or the use of an idiomatic expression may be found. For example, 且 *ch'ieh* is defined in the vocabulary as *conj.* and; but a reference to note 218 gives us the additional information that it only links clauses, not nouns. Where convenient these references to the notes are divided up and attached to the appropriate function and meaning ascribed to the word.

6.   In the case of words of some grammatical interest I list the places in the text-passages where they are to be found. It does not seem necessary to do this for words which occur very frequently, so I have not done so for words which occur more than forty times.

7.   To the left of each character I give the radical number and the number of additional strokes, and to its right I record in brackets the number of occurrences in the text-passages.

8.   In order that this vocabulary may be used as a key to all the grammatical information contained in the book I have included words which are treated in Appendix A as well as those which occur in the text-passages.

9.   The following abbreviations are used:

adj.	adjective	*demonstr.*	demonstrative	*prep.*	preposition
adv.	adverb	*g.s.*	grammatical	*pron.*	pronoun
app.	appendix		survey	*v.*	verb
aux.	auxiliary	*interrog.*	interrogative	*v.i.*	intransitive verb
conj.	conjunction	*n.*	noun	*v.t*	transitive verb

RADICAL 1

1/0	一	(9)	i¹ *n.*, *adj.* one; whole; *v.t.* unify (*verbal noun* unification); *adv.* once; *conj.* once, when once, as soon as; used in 一夫 i¹ fu¹, *n.* private individual, commoner, outcast. 28r, 56k, 56w, 57e, 58i, 60g, 60k, 98t, 106r.
1/1	七	(2)	ch'i¹ *n.*, *adj.* seven, seventh.
1/2	三	(5)	san¹ *n.*, *adj.* three, third.
1/2	上	(8)	shang⁴ *n.* top; superiors; *adj.* upper; first (in a list of two or three) (note 177); *postposition* on, above (notes 65, 83); *v.i.* rise; *v.t.* mount. 3l, 24t, 61u, 89m, 97o, 128m, 128q, 131z.
1/2	下	(28)	hsia⁴ *n.* bottom; inferiors; *adj.* lower; second or third (in list of two or three) (note 177); *postposition* below, under (note 65); *v.i.* descend; *v.t.* dismount from. 3m, 20q, 25a, 56c, 56r, 57m, 58a, 58q, 59j, 65d, 68g, 68t, 77e, 77j, 78b, 80a, 82h, 83e, 88b, 91w, 92b, 94f, 96s, 98m, 102r, 103p, 128i, 128r.
1/3	不	(105)	pu⁴ *adv.* not; *privative prefix* un-, in- (*g.s.* B, notes 3, 20, 58, 152).

90

1/3	丑	(3)	**ch'ou³** *n.* one of the 'twelve branches', a set of characters used in conjunction with the 'ten stems' to form a series or cycle of sixty for numbering days and years.
1/4	世	(3)	**shih⁴** *n.* generation, epoch; *adj.* hereditary (note 212).
1/4	且	(7)	**ch'ieh³** *conj.* and, moreover (notes 218, 289, 318); *aux. v.* be about to, shall (app. A). 85a, 116k, 122v, 129t, 132i, 133q, 139w.
1/4	丘	(8)	**ch'iu¹** *n.* hillock; Confucius's personal name.
1/8	並		**ping⁴** see Appendix A.

RADICAL 2

2/3	中	(2)	**chung¹** *n.* middle; *adj.* central; second of three (note 238). **chung⁴** *v.t.* hit the centre, hit the target. 98a, 100d.

RADICAL 3

3/3	丹	(1)	**tan¹** *n.* cinnabar.
3/4	主	(6)	**chu³** *n.* lord, master; *v.t.* lord it over, preside over; regard as of most importance, lay special emphasis on.

RADICAL 4

4/1	乃	(5)	**nai³** *adv., conj.* thus (note 278); then, thereupon; indeed, really (note 103); used in 無乃 wu² nai³, q.v.; *pron.* your. 32e, 87k, 105r, 116g, 122q.
4/3	之	(159)	**chih¹** *pron.* him, her, it, them (notes 53, 59, 82, 197); *v.t.* go to (note 84); *possessive or determinative particle* (g.s. A.1, notes 15, 34, 323).
4/4	乏	(1)	**fa²** *v.t.* lack; *v.i.* be exhausted; *n.* need, requirement.
4/4	乎	(16)	**hu¹** *interrog. particle* concluding formal interrogative sentences (g.s. D, note 7); *prep.* used for 於 yü², q.v. (note 102). 1w, 21o, 22u, 23x, 31p, 36i, 44k, 45u, 47v, 51x, 55i, 107j, 114s, 127p, 128h, 131i.
4/9	乘	(5)	**ch'eng²** *v.t.* mount, ride, avail oneself of. **ch'eng⁴** *n.* chariot, team of four horses, set of four.

RADICAL 5

5/1	九	(3)	**chiu³** *n., adj.* nine, ninth.
5/2	也	(74)	**yeh³** *particle* which (a) follows predicate of non-verbal sentence (note 34); (b) marks off 'psychological subject' from rest of sentence (notes 28, 323); (c) terminates verbal sentences of a judgemental or explanatory character (notes 25, 46); used in 也已 yeh³ i³ (note 328). See also *g.s.* A.2.
5/7	乳	(1)	**ju³** *v.t.* suckle.

5/12   亂   (2)   **luan⁴** *n.* disorder, confusion, turmoil, rebellion; *v.i.* be in disorder; *v.t.* bring into disorder, cause confusion in.

RADICAL 6

6/3   予   (1)   **yü²** *personal pron.* I, me (note 132).
yü³ *v.* (used for 與) give, allow.
42r.

6/7   事   (3)   **shih⁴** *n.* affair, business; *v.t.* serve.

RADICAL 7

7/0   二   (2)   **erh⁴** *n., adj.* two, second.

7/1   于   **yü²** see Appendix A.

7/2   云   (1)   **yün²** *v.* say (often introducing quotation); *particle* marking end of quotation (note 151).
51q.

7/2   五   (5)   **wu³** *n., adj.* five, fifth.

RADICAL 8

8/1   亡   (6)   **wang²** *v.t.* lose; ruin, destroy; *v.i.* be lost, be ruined, disappear, be in exile, perish; *adj.* abandoned.

8/4   交   (2)   **chiao¹** *v.t.* exchange, contact, have relations with; *pronominal adv.* with each other, mutually (note 14).
3n, 11n.

8/4   亦   (14)   **i⁴** *adv.* also, too, likewise, consequently (notes 4, 43).
1p, 2g, 6l, 8i, 11s, 54x, 68y, 107o, 125n, 127n, 129c, 130e, 136r, 139s.

RADICAL 9

9/0   人   (58)   **jen²** *n.* man; *pron.* someone (note 139); others (note 325).

9/2   今   (12)   **chin¹** *adv.* now; *conj.* if now, if; *adj.* present; *n.* now, the present (notes 110, 136, 269).
34x, 45n, 45z, 47h, 81t, 84q, 99d, 105h, 112n, 114d, 135m, 136c.

9/2   介   (1)   **chieh⁴** *n.* armour; *v.t.* protect.

9/2   仁   (13)   **jen²** *n.* humaneness, benevolence, goodness; *adj.* humane, benevolent, good; *v.i.* be humane.

9/3   以   (77)   **i³** *n.* means; *verb-prep.* using, by means of, in accordance with (notes 85, 148, 154, 183); *conj.* in order to, so as to (note 161); because of (notes 283, 320); used in 以 . . . 為 i³ . . . wei², to regard as (notes 90, 114); in 是以 shih⁴ i³, therefore; in 何以 ho² i³, how?; in 以來 i³ lai², onwards, to the present; in 以後 i³ hou⁴, afterwards. See also *g.s.* A.3, note 6.

9/3   他   (1)   **t'a¹** *pron., adj.* other, another.
34m.

9/4	仲	(2)	**chung⁴** *n.* second in order of birth; used in 仲尼 Chung-ni, the courtesy-name of Confucius.
9/4	伐	(2)	**fa²** *v.t.* strike, attack.
9/4	休	(2)	**hsiu¹** *v.i. & t.* rest.
9/5	作	(2)	**tso⁴** *v.t.* make; *v.i.* arise, operate, be active.
9/5	余		**yü²** see Appendix A.
9/5	何	(29)	**ho²** *interrog. pron. & adj.* what?; *interrog. adv.* how?, why?; used in 何以 ho² i³, how? (*g.s.* D, notes 8, 34, 100). 2c, 2p, 2x, 3g, 6s, 11h, 19w, 22x, 24c, 25h, 26p, 28p, 30u, 31c, 35s, 38o, 46e, 50k, 51j, 69a, 71q, 74c, 84y, 106l, 115b, 115i, 130j, 140w.
9/5	佚	(1)	**i⁴** *adj.* lazy (佚之狐 is the name of a Cheng official).
9/5	伯	(4)	**po²** *n.* eldest in a series of brothers; third in the series of titles of the ancient nobility 公侯伯子男, often translated 'earl'.
9/6	來	(9)	**lai²** *v.i.* come; *adj.* the coming, next; used in 以來 i³ lai², q.v.
9/6	使	(21)	**shih³** *v.t.* send, command, cause (note 244); *conj.* (cause it to be that), suppose that, if. **shih⁴** *n.* envoy.
9/7	侵	(1)	**ch'in¹** *v.t.* raid, encroach upon.
9/7	保	(3)	**pao³** *v.t.* preserve, protect.
9/7	侮	(1)	**wu³** *v.t.* insult.
9/7	侯	(11)	**hou²** *n.* nobleman; second in series of titles of ancient nobility 公侯伯子男, often translated 'marquis'.
9/7	信	(2)	**hsin⁴** *n.* good faith; *v.t.* have faith in, trust; *adj.* sincere, truthful.
9/8	倫	(1)	**lun²** *n.* natural relationship, right principle.
9/8	俱		**chü⁴** see Appendix A.
9/8	倉	(4)	**ts'ang¹** *n.* granary.
9/8	倖	(1)	**hsing⁴** *n.* luck, fortune; *adj.* lucky.
9/9	假	(1)	**chia³** *v.t.* simulate; borrow; *adj.* simulated, false.
9/9	偕	(1)⟩	**chieh¹** *adv.* together (note 314). 131l.
9/11	傳	(1)	**ch'uan²** *v.t.* hand on, transmit. **chuan⁴** *n.* record, tradition.
9/11	傷	(1)	**shang¹** *v.t.* hurt, injure; *n.* harm.
9/12	僞	(1)	**wei⁴** *n.* deceit; *adj.* deceitful; *v.t.* pretend, simulate, cheat.
9/13	儆	(1)	**ching³** *v.t.* warn, put on guard.
9/15	優	(1)	**yu¹** *adj.* liberal, indulgent; *n.* amusement; actor.

RADICAL 10

10/3	兄	(6)	**hsiung¹** *n.* elder brother.
10/4	光	(1)	**kuang¹** *n.* brightness; *adj.* bright; *v.t.* illumine.

10/4 先 (12) **hsien¹** *adj.* preceding, former; *adv.* first.
hsien⁴ *v.t.* precede, pay first visit to; give precedence to, put first.

10/5 克 (1) **k'o⁴** *v.t.* overcome, vanquish.

RADICAL 11

11/0 入 (5) **ju⁴** *v.t.* enter; *adv.* within, at home.

11/2 内 (4) **nei⁴** *postposition* within; *adv.* within, inside, at home; *n.* the inside; *adj.* inner.

11/6 兩 (1) **liang³** *n., adj.* two (note 233).

RADICAL 12

12/0 入 (1) **pa¹** *n., adj.* eight, eighth.

12/2 公 (18) **kung¹** *n.* first in series of titles of ancient nobility 公侯伯子男, often translated 'duke'; *adj.* public.

12/4 共 (2) **kung⁴** *v.t.* join in, share; *adv.* jointly; *v.t.* used for 供 kung¹, supply used for 恭 kung¹, respect.

12/5 兵 (5) **ping¹** *n.* weapon; soldier (N.B. in Mencius it always means weapon).

12/6 其 (64) **ch'i²** *pron.* his, her, its, their (note 17); *adj.* such, so much (app. A); *aux. v.* will (notes 256, 279).

12/8 兼 (2) **chien¹** *v.t.* unite, combine, embrace; *adj.* all-embracing.

RADICAL 13

13/4 再 (3) **tsai⁴** *adv.* twice, a second time.

RADICAL 14

14/7 冠 (3) **kuan¹** *n.* cap.
kuan⁴ *v.t.* cap (in coming-of-age ceremony); wear a cap.

RADICAL 15

15/3 冬 (1) **tung¹** *n.* winter.

RADICAL 16

16/1 凡 (3) **fan²** *adj.* all (note 236).
96q, 98p, 110n.

RADICAL 17

17/2 凶 (2) **hsiung¹** *v.i.* be in distress, suffer calamity; *adj.* disastrous, inauspicious.

17/3 出 (6) **ch'u¹** *v.i.* go out; *v.t.* leave; issue, emit, drive out; *adv.* outside, abroad.

17/6 函 (1)   **han²** *v.t.* contain, envelop; *n.* armour; used in 函陵 Hanling, a place in Cheng.

RADICAL 18

18/1 刃 (1)   **jen⁴** *n.* edge of weapon, blade, weapon, sword.

18/2 分 (3)   **fen¹** *v.t.* divide, share.
fen⁴ *n.* division, share, lot.

18/5 利 (16)   **li⁴** *adj.* sharp; *v.t.* profit, benefit; *n.* profit, advantage.

18/5 初   **ch'u¹** see Appendix A.

18/6 刺 (1)   **tz'u⁴** *v.t.* stab.

18/7 前 (8)   **ch'ien²** *adj.* previous, former; *adv.* previously; *v.i.* come forward; *postposition* before, in front of (note 155); *n.* front.
36w, 38f, 38v, 39c, 52l, 88c, 94p, 95w.

18/7 削 (1)   **hsüeh⁴** *v.t.* pare off, scrape away, annex.

18/7 則 (19)   **tse²** *n.* model, law; *v.t.* model oneself on, imitate; *conj.* accordingly, then (notes 30, 144).
7s, 11q, 12a, 19o, 22s, 22z, 26j, 30r, 34q, 48z, 49d, 51s, 69m, 81j, 86b, 86g, 96d, 96i, 122h.

18/13 劍 (1)   **chien⁴** *n.* sword.

RADICAL 19

19/0 力 (3)   **li⁴** *n.* strength.

19/3 加 (2)   **chia¹** *v.t.* add, apply, bestow; *adv.* increasingly, more (note 33).
9c, 9j.

19/3 功 (7)   **kung¹** *n.* achievement, success, merit.

19/7 勇 (1)   **yung³** *n.* bravery; *adj.* brave.

19/10 勝 (9)   **sheng⁴** *v.t.* overcome, defeat, be victorious.
sheng¹ *adv.* completely (in 不可勝 pu⁴ k'o³ sheng¹, see note 49).

19/10 勞 (1)   **lao²** *n.* toil, labour; *v.t.* toil, labour, work for.
lao⁴ *n.*, *v.t.* reward.

RADICAL 20

20/2 勿 (3)   **wu⁴** *adv.* (used for 母之) do not . . . it; not . . .it (notes 57, 272).
16q, 114o, 119n.

RADICAL 21

21/3 北 (3)   **pei³** *n.*, *adj.* north, northern.

RADICAL 23

23/2 匹夫 (4)   **p'i³ fu¹** *n.* ordinary man, private individual, commoner.

RADICAL 24

24/0	十	(9)	**shih²** *n., adj.* ten, tenth.
24/1	千	(6)	**ch'ien¹** *n., adj.* thousand.
24/2	升	(2)	**sheng¹** *n.* a measure (sometimes translated 'pint').
24/2	午	(1)	**wu³** *n.* one of the 'twelve branches' (cf. 1/3 丑 ch'ou³).
24/3	半	(1)	**pan⁴** *n., adj.* half.
24/6	卒	(3)	**tsu²** *n.* soldier, group; *v.i.* die, finish; *v.t.* complete; *adv.* finally.
24/7	南	(4)	**nan²** *n., adj.,* south, southern.

RADICAL 26

| 26/4 | 危 | (2) | **wei¹** *adj.* lofty, precipitous, dangerous; *n.* danger; *v.i.* be in danger; *v.t.* endanger. |
| 26/7 | 即 | (1) | **chi²** *v.t.* come to, reach; *adv.* at that moment (note 94); *conj.* then. 28t. |

RADICAL 27

| 27/7 | 厚 | (5) | **hou⁴** *adj.* thick, ample, generous; *n.* abundance; *v.t.* enrich, strengthen. |
| 27/12 | 厭 | (1) | **yen⁴** *n.* satiety. |

RADICAL 28

| 28/3 | 去 | (1) | **ch'ü⁴** *v.t.* go away, leave, escape. |
| | | | **ch'ü³** *v.t.* remove, get rid of. |

RADICAL 29

29/0	又	(4)	**yu⁴** *adv., conj.* and, furthermore, also (notes 284, 308, 338). 120v, 123v, 129q, 141e.
29/2	反	(2)	**fan³** *v.i.* return, go back; *v.t.* turn, return, restore, pay back; *adv.* backwards.
29/2	友	(1)	**yu³** *n.* friend; *v.t.* befriend, associate with.
29/2	及	(2)	**chi²** *v.t.* reach, arrive at, attain; *prep.* (arriving at), by, until; *conj.* when; and, together with (app. A).
29/6	叔	(1)	**shu²** *n.* third of four brothers.
29/6	受	(1)	**shou⁴** *v.t.* receive, accept.
29/6	取	(5)	**ch'ü³** *v.t.* take, seize.
29/8	叟	(1)	**sou³** *n.* old man.

RADICAL 30

| 30/0 | 口 | (1) | **k'ou³** *n.* mouth. |
| 30/2 | 可 | (35) | **k'o³** *aux. v.* can, be able, may, should (*g.s.* E, notes 55, 75, 77, 81, 286). |

11l, 12q, 13d, 13r, 14a, 14g, 15p, 16h, 16y, 21l, 23a, 23t, 24a, 24g, 26q, 43v, 44e, 45t, 57r, 59o, 60u, 75b, 75l, 75t, 76b, 76m, 114r, 115k, 117i, 118b, 118k, 119j, 122c, 122r, 123x.

30/2	司	(2)	**ssu**[1] *v.t.* superintend; *n.* office.
30/2	右	(1)	**yu**[4] *n.* right-hand side, occupant of right-hand position in chariot; *adj.* right-hand.
30/3	同	(2)	**t'ung**[2] *adv.* together; *v.i.* be the same; *v.t.* share, partake in, join; *n.* similarity.
30/3	各		**ko**[4] see Appendix A.
30/3	名	(2)	**ming**[2] *n.* name, reputation; *v.t.* name, call.
30/4	否	(4)	**fou**[3] *proclausal negative* no, or not (note 121). 39n, 47u, 114k, 123y.
30/4	吾	(22)	**wu**[2] *personal pron.* I, my (notes 62, 130). 1u, 2s, 3a, 3j, 24f, 25t, 28o, 42c, 62m, 62y, 69n, 72z, 73p, 96b, 104m, 107r, 114e, 119p, 123d, 132g, 135w.
30/4	告	(3)	**kao**[4] *v.t.* tell, report, announce.
30/4	吳	(7)	**wu**[2] *n.* name of an ancient Chinese state.
30/4	君	(45)	**chün**[1] *n.* ruler, lord; *quasi-pron.* you, sir (note 252).
30/5	命	(4)	**ming**[4] *n.* order, instruction, command, decree of heaven, fate; *v.t.* instruct, command.
30/5	和	(1)	**ho**[2] *n.* harmony; *v.i.* be at peace, be harmonious; *v.t.* calm, reconcile.
30/6	哉	(10)	**tsai**[1] *particle* (generally final) expressing surprise (notes 79, 131, 149). 23y, 31e, 35t, 38p, 42u, 54m, 64u, 69t, 84z, 114l.
30/8	問	(2)	**wen**[4] *v.t.* ask, enquire about; *n.* question.
30/8	唯	(3)	**wei**[2] *adv.* only (note 340). 116y, 125y, 141x.
30/9	喻	(1)	**yü**[4] *v.t.* understand, illustrate.
30/9	喜	(1)	**hsi**[3] *v.i.* be glad, rejoice.
30/9	喪	(7)	**sang**[4] *v.t.* lose, destroy. **sang**[1] *n.* mourning; *v.t.* mourn.
30/9	善	(3)	**shan**[4] *n.* goodness; *adj.* good; *v.i.* be good. **shan**[3] *v.t.* approve, cause to be good.
30/11	嘗	(2)	**ch'ang**[2] *v.t.* taste, experience; *aux. v.* have, have once, once (note 164). 55s, 139y.

RADICAL 31

31/2	四	(1)	**ssu**[4] *n.* four; *adj.* four, fourth, on all four sides (note 290).
31/3	因		**yin**[1] see Appendix A.
31/4	困	(1)	**k'un**[4] *n.* distress, exhaustion.
31/5	固	(3)	**ku**[4] *adj.* strong, secure, firm; *v.t.* strengthen; *adv.* certainly, absolutely (note 194).

31/8	國	(24)	**kuo²** *n.* state, country, capital city.
31/9	圍	(2)	**wei²** *v.t.* encircle, besiege.
31/11	圖	(5)	**t'u²** *v.t.* consider, make plans about.

RADICAL 32

32/3	在	(1)	**tsai⁴** *v.t.* be at, be in, be on, consist in, depend on; *v.i.* be alive, be present.
32/3	地	(5)	**ti⁴** *n.* earth, land, territory, place.
32/4	坐	(1)	**tso⁴** *v.i.* sit; *v.t.* take up a position at.
32/6	城	(2)	**ch'eng²** *n.* city wall, city; *v.t.* fortify.
32/8	執	(2)	**chih²** *v.t.* seize, grasp; used in 執事 chih² shih⁴, officer (note 333).
32/8	堂	(2)	**t'ang²** *n.* hall.
32/8	堅	(1)	**chien¹** *adj.* tough, solid, strong.
32/9	堯	(1)	**yao¹** *n.* name of a legendary emperor of antiquity.
32/10	塗	(1)	**t'u²** *n.* mud, road.
32/10	填	(1)	**t'ien²** used for sound of drum (note 37).
32/12	墨	(12)	**mo⁴** *n.* name of ancient Chinese philosopher.

RADICAL 33

| 33/0 | 士 | (8) | **shih⁴** *n.* officer, minor official, scholar, knight. |
| 33/4 | 壯 | (1) | **chuang⁴** *adj.* strong, able-bodied. |

RADICAL 35

| 35/7 | 夏 | (1) | **hsia⁴** *n.* summer; name of dynasty. |

RADICAL 36

36/0	夕	(2)	**hsi²** *n.* evening.
36/2	外	(3)	**wai⁴** *adv.* outside, abroad; *adj.* outer, outside, external.
36/3	多	(10)	**to¹** *adj.* many; *adv.* numerously (note 230); *v.i.* be numerous; *v.t.* make much of. 5f, 9k, 12f, 65w, 66g, 67p, 68a, 68z, 90z, 124b.
36/5	夜	(3)	**yeh⁴** *n.* night.

RADICAL 37

| 37/0 | 大 | (15) | **ta⁴** *adj.* great; *n.* greatness; *adv.* greatly; *v.i.* be great; *v.t.* enlarge; used in 大夫 tai⁴ fu¹, high official, grandee; used in 大山 t'ai⁴ shan¹, Mt. T'ai. |
| 37/1 | 夫 | (15) | **fu¹** *n.* man; used in 一夫 i¹ fu¹ and 大夫 tai⁴ fu¹, qq.v. |

fu² *demonstr. adj.* this (notes 190, 206); *pron.* this person, he (note 259); *interrog. final particle* used for 否乎 fou³ hu¹ (app. A).
2v, 36d, 39b 6oh, 6ol, 62c, 62s, 68i, 71o, 8od, 89r, 1o6y, 112o, 122w, 14ou.

37/1	天	(22)	**t'ien¹** *n.* heaven, sky.
37/2	失	(2)	**shih¹** *v.t.* lose, neglect.
37/5	奈	(1)	**nai⁴** see note 217.
37/7	奚	(1)	**hsi¹** *interrog. pron.* what? (note 117). 37m.
37/11	奪	(2)	**to²** *v.t.* snatch, deprive.

RADICAL 38

38/0	女	(2)	**nü³** *n.* woman, girl, daughter. **ju³** (used for 汝) *personal pron.* you (note 313). 78r, 131k.
38/3	妄	(2)	**wang⁴** *adj.* lawless, reckless.
38/3	如	(15)	**ju²** *v.t.* be as good as, be like, do like (notes 42, 157, 176, 312); go to; *prep.* like; *conj.* if (note 44). See also *g.s.* F. 8q, 11i, 11x, 22y, 43m, 46c, 52q, 85h, 85l, 89i, 95q, 99v, 99z, 131q, 135k.
38/3	好	(3)	**hao³** *adj.* good. **hao⁴** *v.t.* love, be fond of.
38/5	始	(3)	**shih³** *n.* beginning; *v.t.* begin; *adv.* in the beginning.
38/5	姓	(6)	**hsing⁴** *n.* surname.
38/5	妾	(2)	**ch'ieh⁴** *n.* concubine.
38/6	姦	(1)	**chien¹** *n.* adultery, lawlessness, treachery, villainy.
38/6	威	(2)	**wei¹** *n.* majesty, dignity; *v.t.* inspire awe in, terrify.
38/8	婦	(2)	**fu⁴** *n.* woman, wife (婦人 fu⁴ jen² also occurs with the same meaning).
38/13	嬖	(2)	**pi⁴** *v.t.* favour; *n., adj.* favourite.

RADICAL 39

39/0	子	(69)	**tzu³** *n.* son, daughter, child; fourth in series of titles of ancient nobility 公侯伯子男, often translated 'viscount'; master (used with names of philosophers); *quasi-pron.* you, sir.
39/1	孔	(9)	**k'ung³** *n.* surname of Confucius.
39/4	孝	(2)	**hsiao⁴** *n.* filial piety.
39/5	孤	(1)	**ku¹** *n.* orphan, lonely one (used to refer to ruler); *adj.* solitary, lonely.
39/5	孟	(11)	**meng⁴** *n.* eldest of brothers; surname of Mencius.
39/5	季	(5)	**chi⁴** *n.* youngest of a series of brothers.
39/7	孫	(1)	**sun¹** *n.* grandson, descendant.

99

| 39/8 | 孰 | (6) | **shu²** *interrog. pron.* which?, who? (notes 181, 267). 65v, 67o, 110z, 111j, 112b, 116u. |

| 39/13 | 學 | (1) | **hsüeh²** *n.* learning; *adj.* learned; *v.t.* study. |

RADICAL 40

| 40/3 | 宅 | (1) | **chai²** *n.* house, homestead. |

| 40/3 | 安 | | **an¹** see Appendix A. |

| 40/3 | 守 | (1) | **shou³** *v.t.* guard, protect. |

| 40/4 | 宋 | (5) | **sung⁴** *n.* name of an ancient Chinese state. |

| 40/5 | 宜 | (1) | **i²** *adj.* right, proper, natural, reasonable. |

| 40/6 | 宣 | (1) | **hsüan¹** *v.t.* spread, proclaim; understand; *n.* king's name. |

| 40/6 | 室 | (1) | **shih⁴** *n.* house. |

| 40/7 | 害 | (4) | **hai⁴** *v.t.* hurt; *n.* harm, damage. |

| 40/7 | 家 | (4) | **chia¹** *n.* clan, family. |

| 40/8 | 宿 | (1) | **su⁴** *v.i.* stay overnight. |

| 40/9 | 寒 | (4) | **han²** *v.i.* be cold; *adj.* cold. |

| 40/9 | 富 | (2) | **fu⁴** *n.* wealth; *adj.* wealthy; *v.t.* enrich. |

| 40/11 | 寡 | (8) | **kua³** *adj.* solitary, few; used in 寡人 kua³ jen², *quasi-pron.* the solitary person, I (note 28). 7e, 8r, 9e, 23q, 37w, 43k, 44g, 136i. |

| 40/11 | 察 | (2) | **ch'a²** *v.t.* perceive, distinguish, examine, investigate. |

| 40/11 | 實 | (2) | **shih²** *n.* fruit, essence, reality; *adj.* full, real, sincere; *adv.* truly; *postposed demonstr. pron.* this (note 299). 120u, 127b. |

| 40/12 | 寬 | (1) | **k'uan¹** *adj.* indulgent, magnanimous. |

| 40/16 | 寵 | (1) | **ch'ung³** *n.*, *v.t.* favour. |

RADICAL 41

| 41/0 | 寸 | (1) | **ts'un⁴** *n.* inch. |

| 41/6 | 封 | (5) | **feng¹** *n.* mound, boundary wall, boundary, fief; *v.t.* invest with a fief, enfeoff. |

| 41/8 | 將 | (21) | **chiang¹** *v.t.* take, lead; *aux. v.* be about to (*g.s.* E, note 5); used in 將軍 chiang⁴ chün¹, *n.* general. 1q, 25l, 34d, 35n, 43c, 43z, 70l, 73x, 84v, 88o, 93i, 99c, 100c, 100u, 101u, 102k, 110c, 119q, 126p, 130s, 141o. |

| 41/9 | 尊 | (1) | **tsun¹** *v.t.* honour. |

| 41/11 | 對 | (9) | **tui⁴** *v.i.* reply |

RADICAL 42

| 42/0 | 小 | (4) | **hsiao³** *adj.* small; *adv.* slightly; *v.t.* make small. |

42/1	少	(4)	**shao³** *adj.* few; *adv.* sparsely (note 182).
			shao⁴ *adj.* young.
			9c, 68n, 76h, 97e.
42/5	尚		**shang⁴** see Appendix A.

RADICAL 43

43/1	尤	(1)	**yu²** *n.* fault; *v.t.* blame.
43/9	就	(4)	**chiu⁴** *v.t.* approach.

RADICAL 44

44/1	尺	(3)	**ch'ih³** *n.* measurement of length, often translated 'foot'.
44/2	尼	(2)	**ni³** *v.t.* stop.
44/7	展	(1)	**chan³** *v.t.* unroll, open, develop.
44/12	履	(1)	**li³** *n.* sandal; tread; *v.t.* tread.

RADICAL 46

46/0	山	(3)	**shan¹** *n.* mountain.

RADICAL 48

48/2	巧	(1)	**ch'iao³** *adj.* artful.

RADICAL 49

49/0	己	(2)	**chi³** *pron.* himself, themselves (note 302).
			127k, 128f.
49/0	已	(5)	**i³** *v.t.* finish; *aux. v.* have, have already (notes 111, 143); used in 而巳 erh² i³ and 也巳 yeh³ i³, qqv.
			2l, 6q, 35a, 48n, 135t.

RADICAL 50

50/2	布	(1)	**pu⁴** *n.* cloth; *v.t.* spread out, display, announce.
50/5	帛	(2)	**po⁴** *n.* silk.
50/7	師	(1)	**shih¹** *n.* army, host; tutor, master; *v.t.* take as teacher, imitate.
50/7	席	(1)	**hsi²** *n.* mat (N.B. in antiquity the Chinese sat on the floor).
50/8	帶	(1)	**tai⁴** *n.* girdle; *v.t.* girdle oneself with.
50/11	幕	(1)	**mu⁴** *n.* tent, screen, curtain.

RADICAL 51

51/2	平	(1)	**p'ing²** *v.i.* be level, be equal, be at peace; *v.t.* pacify, reconcile.
51/5	幸	(2)	**hsing⁴** *n.* luck, fortune, favour; *adj.* lucky, fortunate.

RADICAL 52

52/9   幾   chi³ see Appendix A.

RADICAL 53

53/4   序   (1)   **hsü⁴** *n.* school.

53/5   庖   (1)   **p'ao²** *n.* kitchen.

53/6   庠   (1)   **hsiang²** *n.* school.

53/8   庶   (1)   **shu⁴** *adj.* numerous, all; used in 庶人 shu⁴ jen² and 庶民 shu⁴ min², the common people.

53/12   廢   (3)   **fei⁴** *v.t.* cast aside, get rid of, dispense with, depose.

53/12   廣   (1)   **kuang³** *adj.* broad, extensive.

53/12   廚   (1)   **ch'u²** *n.* kitchen.

53/13   廩   (2)   **lin³** *n.* granary.

RADICAL 56

56/10   弒   (2)   **shih⁴** *v.t.* assassinate.

RADICAL 57

57/1   弔   (3)   **tiao⁴** *v.t.* condole, comfort, pay visit of condolence.

57/2   弗   (4)   **fu²** *adv.* (used for 不之 pu⁴ chih¹) not . . . it (note 185). 69c, 82k, 118h, 1250.

57/4   弟   (9)   **ti⁴** *n.* younger brother.

57/9   強   (2) }   **ch'iang²** *adj.* strong.

57/13   彊   (2)   **ch'iang³** *v.t.* compel.

RADICAL 58

58/9   彘   (2)   **chih⁴** *n.* pig.

RADICAL 60

60/5   往   (5)   **wang³** *v.i.* go; *n.* going.

60/5   彼   (3)   **pi³** *demonstr. adj.* that; *pron.* that person, those people, he, they (note 96). 30d, 110b, 115v.

60/6   後   (12)   **hou⁴** *adj.* later; rear; *adv.* later, afterwards; behind, in the rear; *v.t.* succeed; put last, relegate; *postposition* behind; *n.* posterity; rear. 5j, 6f, 10q, 10x, 22g, 36t, 38c, 38y, 39h, 56i, 58g, 60e.

60/7   徒   (5)   **t'u²** *n.* foot-soldier, follower, partisan; *adv.* only, merely (app. A).

60/8   從   (4)   **ts'ung²** *v.t.* follow, pursue, comply, agree to; *prep.* from (note 195).

tsung⁴ *n.* follower.
73q, 77t, 125d, 135a.

60/8	御	(2)	yü⁴ *v.t.* drive a chariot, direct, govern, manage; *n.* charioteer.
60/8	得	(15)	te² *v.t.* get, obtain, catch; *aux. v.* succeed in, manage to, be able to (*g.s.* E, notes 135, 143). 21m, 44i, 48m, 56v, 57d, 58u, 59b, 69b, 69g, 75z, 78t, 93x, 111q, 115w, 116c, 123s.
60/9	復	(2)	fu⁴ *v.t.* report, repay, reply, restore, return to, repeat; *adv.* again.
60/9	徧		pien⁴ see Appendix A.
60/10	微		wei¹ see Appendix A.
60/12	德	(6)	te² *n.* mana, virtue, moral power, goodness, quality; *v.t.* regard as a virtue, be grateful for.
60/13	徼	(1)	chiao¹ *v.t.* seek.

RADICAL 61

61/0	心	(9)	hsin¹ *n.* mind, heart, feelings.
61/1	必	(20)	pi⁴ *aux. v.* must, be bound to, make a point of; *adv.* always, certainly; *v.t.* be bound to get (*g.s.* E, notes 18, 142). 2d, 4c, 4p, 6t, 34r, 48e, 62p, 63b, 80i, 80r, 83o, 83x, 86p, 105n, 113p, 118t, 118z, 122n, 126o, 134x.
61/3	忘	(1)	wang⁴ *v.t.* forget.
61/3	忍	(6)	jen³ *v.t.* endure.
61/3	志	(2)	chih⁴ *n.* will, purpose, ambition; *v.t.* record.
61/4	忠	(1)	chung¹ *n.* loyalty; *adj.* loyal.
61/5	怨	(1)	yüan⁴ *n.* resentment; *v.t.* resent; *adj.* resentful.
61/5	怒	(3)	nu⁴ *v.i.* be angry; *adj.* angry.
61/5	急	(1)	chi² *n.* urgency, exigency, stress; *v.i.* be in distress.
61/6	恩	(1)	en¹ *n.* kindness.
61/6	恐	(1)	k'ung³ *v.t.* fear.
61/6	恤	(2)	hsü⁴ *v.t.* pity, care about, sympathize with.
61/6	耴	(1)	ch'ih³ *n.* shame, disgrace; *v.i.* feel ashamed.
61/7	患	(1)	huan⁴ *n.* distress, calamity; *v.t.* regard as a calamity, be anxious about.
61/7	悅	(1)	yüeh⁴ *v.i.* be pleased.
61/7	悍	(1)	han⁴ *adj.* cruel, violent, fierce.
61/7	悌	(2)	t'i⁴ *n.* respect towards an elder brother.
61/8	惡	(5)	wu⁴ *v.t.* hate; *n.* hatred. o⁴ *n., adj.* bad, evil. wu¹ *interrog. adv.* how?, where? (note 97); *interjection* oh! (note 147). 30e, 50i, 110d, 111f, 113f.
61/8	惠	(6)	hui⁴ *adj.* kind; *v.t.* be kind to, cherish; *n.* kindness.

61/8	惑	(3)	**huo⁴** *v.t.* doubt; mislead, delude; *n.* delusion.
61/9	愈	(2)	**yü⁴** *v.i.* be better, recover, be superior, surpass; *adv.* more.
61/9	愛	(9)	**ai⁴** *v.t.* love; grudge; *n.* love.
61/9	意	(3)	**i⁴** *n.* thought, idea; *v.t.* think.
61/10	慈	(1)	**tz'u²** *v.t.* be kind, deal kindly with; *n.* kindness.
61/11	憂	(2)	**yu¹** *n.* sadness, sorrow, suffering; *v.t.* sorrow over, feel pity for.
61/11	慮	(9)	**lü⁴** *v.t.* think of, be anxious about; *n.* thoughts.
61/12	憚	(1)	**tan⁴** *v.t.* dislike, dread.
61/13	憾	(2)	**han⁴** *n.* resentment, dissatisfaction.
61/14	懟	(1)	**tui⁴** *v.i.* feel resentment.
61/16	懷	(1)	**huai²** *v.t.* cherish.
61/18	懼	(3)	**chü⁴** *v.t.* be afraid, fear.

RADICAL 62

| 62/2 | 成 | (1) | **ch'eng²** *v.t.* achieve, complete, finish, bring to terms, reconcile. |
| 62/3 | 我 | (16) | **wo³** *personal pron.* I, me (note 62). |

19r, 20g, 31f, 31w, 47p, 51z, 52r, 90d, 93h, 105m, 106o, 117l, 118n, 118y, 119c, 120e.

| 62/4 | 或 | (6) | **huo⁴** *pron.* someone, some (notes 39, 128); *adv.* perhaps (或者 huo⁴ che³ also occurs with the same meaning) (note 136). |

10m, 10s, 37u, 41o, 41s, 45q.

| 62/12 | 戰 | (7) | **chan⁴** *n.* battle, warfare; *v.i.* fight a battle. |
| 62/14 | 戴 | (1) | **tai⁴** *v.t.* carry on the head, bear, support. |

RADICAL 63

| 63/0 | 戶 | (2) | **hu⁴** *n.* door, household. |
| 63/4 | 所 | (16) | **so³** *n.* place; *relative pron.* what, that which (*g.s.* A.6, notes 109, 112, 118, 129, 198, 204, 251, 335–6). |

34v, 35h, 35v, 38r, 39y, 41z, 50c, 54t, 74s, 74x, 79g, 95y, 105e, 116e, 139u, 140r.

RADICAL 64

64/0	手	(1)	**shou³** *n.* hand.
64/0	才	(2)	**ts'ai²** *n.* talent, ability; *adj.* talented.
64/5	拜	(3)	**pai⁴** *v.t.* do obeisance, bow, acknowledge, give thanks.
64/6	指	(1)	**chih³** *n.* finger, toe; *v.t.* point, indicate.
64/8	授	(2)	**shou⁴** *v.t.* give, offer.
64/8	接	(1)	**chieh¹** *v.t.* connect, come into contact, receive.
64/8	推	(2)	**t'ui¹** *v.t.* push, extend.

64/10	搖	(1)	**yao²** *v.t.* shake.
64/11	摳	(1)	**k'ou¹** *v.t.* raise, pull up.
64/13	擅	(1)	**shan⁴** *v.i.* act on one's own authority, take it upon oneself to.
64/13	擇	(1)	**tse²** *v.t.* choose.

RADICAL 66

66/2	收	(1)	**shou¹** *v.t.* receive, take, gather.
66/3	攻	(4)	**kung¹** *v.t.* attack, apply oneself to.
66/5	故	(9)	**ku⁴** *n.* cause, reason; *conj.* therefore (notes 95, 255). 29g, 52m, 63d, 69b, 105u, 108v, 109s, 117b, 124k.
66/5	政	(7)	**cheng⁴** *n.* government.
66/6	效	(1)	**hsiao⁴** *v.t.* follow, approach, imitate.
66/7	教	(11)	**chiao⁴** *v.t.* teach, instruct; *n.* education.
66/7	救	(1)	**chiu⁴** *v.t.* rescue, relieve, go to the relief of.
66/7	敗	(1)	**pai⁴** *v.i.* be defeated; *v.t.* cause to be defeated, defeat.
66/8	敝		**pi⁴** see Appendix A.
66/8	敢	(5)	**kan³** *aux. v.* dare to, venture to, presume to (note 332). 35j, 52g, 98g, 109u, 137x.
66/9	敬	(7)	**ching⁴** *n.* respect; *v.t.* respect.
66/11	敵	(1)	**ti²** *n.* enemy; *v.t.* be a match for, oppose.
66/11	數	(5)	**shu⁴** *n.* number; *adj.* several. **shu³** *v.t.* count, tick off, reprimand. **ts'u⁴** *adj.* fine, close.

RADICAL 67

| 67/0 | 文 | (5) | **wen²** *n.* markings, lines, ornament, written character, writing, embellishment, literature; name of father of founder of Chou Dynasty; *adj.* cultured, civil (as opposed to military); *v.t.* embellish. |
| 67/8 | 斑 | (1) | **pan¹** *adj.* variegated, mottled. |

RADICAL 69

69/0	斤	(1)	**chin¹** *n.* axe.
69/4	斧	(1)	**fu³** *n.* axe.
69/8	斯	(1)	**ssu¹** *demonstr. adj. & pron.* this; *conj.* then (note 64). 200.

RADICAL 70

| 70/0 | 方 | (3) | **fang¹** *n.* square, quarter, region; method; *adj.* square, local; *conj.* while, so long as, at the moment when (app. A); *adv.* at that moment, |

then (note 223).
71z, 73s, 87l.

70/4	於	(38)	**yü²** *prep.* in, on, at, among, from; than; by (*g.s.* A.7, notes 47, 253). 7h, 7w, 8c, 12g, 17v, 19y, 24r, 29q, 32r, 36b, 40q, 45a, 47n, 48a, 48j, 52j, 53p, 63u, 69k, 70v, 71e, 74k, 74p, 92p, 93z, 105a, 105l, 105y, 107g, 111g, 113s, 114c, 118x, 121k, 133o, 133s, 134h, 137v.
70/5	施	(1)	**shih¹** *v.t.* bestow; do.
70/7	旌	(1)	**ching¹** *n.* banner; *v.t.* distinguish, mark.

RADICAL 71

71/0	无		see 86/8
71/5	既	(6)	**chi⁴** *aux. v.* have, have already (note 38). 10e, 57q, 59n, 60t, 137l, 141a.

RADICAL 72

72/0	日	(6)	**jih⁴** *n.* sun, day.
72/2	早	(1)	**tsao³** *adv.* early.
72/4	昔	(3)	**hsi¹** *adv.* formerly, in ancient times (昔者 hsi¹ che³ also occurs with the same meaning) (note 136). 45i, 45w, 46t.
72/4	易	(5)	**i⁴** *v.t.* change, exchange, replace; *adj.* easy, negligent, frivolous.
72/4	明	(2)	**ming²** *adj.* bright, intelligent, illustrious; *n.* brightness, eye-sight; *v.t.* exhibit, illustrate; used in 明日 ming² jih⁴, next day.
72/4	昆	(1)	**k'un¹** *n.* elder brother.
72/5	星	(1)	**hsing¹** *n.* star.
72/5	是	(20)	**shih⁴** *demonstr. pron. & adj.* this (notes 45, 266); used in 是以 shih⁴ i³, therefore (notes 70, 106); *adj.* right, correct; *n.* right. 11r, 14j, 19v, 22e, 27f, 31a, 32d, 33l, 38h, 41g, 50j, 51i, 51y, 91r, 110q, 117q, 124j, 130y, 131h, 136h.
72/6	晉	(13)	**chin⁴** *n.* name of an ancient Chinese state.
72/6	時	(4)	**shih²** *n.* time, season; *adj.* timely, seasonable.
72/7	晚	(1)	**wan³** *adj.* late.
72/7	晝	(1)	**chou⁴** *n.* day, daytime.
72/8	景	(2)	**ching³** *adj.* bright, splendid.
72/8	智	(1)	**chih⁴** *n.* wisdom.
72/11	暴	(1)	**pao⁴** *v.t.* oppress, tyrannize over; *adj.* violent, oppressive.

RADICAL 73

73/0	曰	(98)	**yüeh⁴** *v.t.* say, mention, mean, name.
73/2	曳	(1)	**i⁴** *v.t.* drag, trail.

73/3	更	(1)	**keng¹** *v.t.* change.
			keng⁴ *adv.* again.

RADICAL 74

74/0	月	(1)	**yüeh⁴** *n.* moon, month.
74/2	有	(36)	**yu³** *v.t.* have, there is/are (notes 26, 126); used in 有司 'yu³ ssu¹, *n.* official (note 108).
			1r, 2h, 5t, 6c, 18t, 19f, 24u, 26z, 27c, 28f, 34t, 35d, 40z, 43r, 44q, 46v, 46y, 53f, 54y, 55d, 55m, 72a, 74f, 74i, 74y, 96t, 98r, 99s, 100w, 105d, 112v, 118e, 126q, 136s, 137t, 140z.
74/4	服	(1)	**fu²** *v.t.* submit to, cause to submit, subdue; wear; *n.* clothes.
74/7	望	(2)	**wang⁴** *v.t.* look from afar towards, gaze at, hope, expect.
74/8	朝	(9)	**chao¹** *n.* morning.
			ch'ao² *n., adj.* court; *v.t.* attend court, cause to attend one's court, give audience to.

RADICAL 75

75/0	木	(3)	**mu⁴** *n.* wood, tree.
75/1	本	(1)	**pen³** *n.* root, source, origin.
75/1	未	(10)	**wei⁴** *adv.* not, not yet, never (*g.s.* B, notes 24–5, 59, 164).
			5s, 6b, 18r, 22m, 32k, 35f, 50a, 106b, 117v, 126l.
75/3	李	(1)	see 144/0.
75/3	材	(2)	**ts'ai²** *n.* timber, material.
75/4	枝	(1)	**chih¹** *n.* branch of tree.
75/4	東	(7)	**tung¹** *n., adj.* east, eastern.
75/4	林	(1)	**lin²** *n.* forest.
75/4	果	(3)	**kuo³** *n.* fruit, result, effect, actuality; *adv.* in effect, in the event, actually (note 127).
			41j, 98f, 121j.
75/5	柳	(4)	**liu³** *n.* willow.
75/6	桓	(3)	**huan²** *n.* name of famous ruler of state of Ch'i; used in 桓叔 Huan Shu, a member of a powerful branch of the Chin ruling family which, after a century of rivalry, had displaced the legitimate line in 678 B.C.
75/6	桑	(1)	**sang¹** *n.* mulberry tree.
75/6	案	(1)	**an⁴** *v.t.* lay hand on, seize.
75/7	梯	(2)	**t'i¹** *n.* ladder, steps.
75/7	械	(1)	**hsieh⁴** *n.* fetters, implement, weapon.
75/7	梁	(2)	**liang²** *n.* bridge, dam; name of an ancient Chinese state.
75/8	極	(1)	**chi²** *n.* ridge of roof, highest point, limit.
75/8	棄	(2)	**ch'i⁴** *v.t.* abandon, reject, throw away.

75/8	棺	(1)	**kuan¹** *n.* inner coffin.
75/8	椁	(1)	**kuo³** *n.* outer coffin.
75/9	楚	(3)	**ch'u³** *n.* name of an ancient Chinese state.
75/11	樂	(2)	**le⁴** *n.* pleasure; *v.t.* take pleasure in.
			yüeh⁴ *n.* music.
75/12	樹	(1)	**shu⁴** *v.t.* plant; *n.* tree.
75/12	橫	(1)	**heng²** *adj.* crosswise.
			heng⁴ *adj.* perverse, unjust.
75/13	檢	(1)	**chien³** *v.t.* control, restrict.

RADICAL 76

76/2	次	(1)	**tz'u⁴** *v.t.* halt; *v.t.* arrange in order; *n.* stopping place, resting place; *adj.* next, second.
76/7	欲	(5)	**yü⁴** *n., aux. v.* wish, desire.
			111x, 112g, 114n, 116b, 141f.

RADICAL 77

77/0	止	(4)	**chih³** *v.i.* stop, remain, desist; *v.t.* stop, detain.
77/1	正	(2)	**cheng⁴** *adj.* straight, correct; principal, chief; *v.t.* regulate, correct.
77/2	此	(8)	**tz'u³** *demonstr. pron. & adj.* this (notes 45, 96).
			11z, 89q, 97n, 97z, 98l, 98s, 99h, 103g.
77/4	步	(8)	**pu⁴** pace; *v.i. & t.* march.
77/4	武	(5)	**wu³** *n.* military power, warlike virtue, martial quality; name of first king of Chou Dynasty; *adj.* martial, warlike.
77/9	歲	(2)	**sui⁴** *n.* year, harvest.
77/14	歸	(2)	**kuei¹** *v.t.* return to, give allegiance to.

RADICAL 78

78/2	死	(12)	**ssu³** *v.i.* die; *v.t.* die with; *n.* the dead, death; *adj.* dead.
78/4	歿	(2)	**mo⁴** *v.i.* die.
78/7	殍	(1)	**p'iao³** *v.i.* die of hunger.

RADICAL 79

79/7	殺	(9)	**sha¹** *v.t.* kill.

RADICAL 80

80/1	母	(4)	**mu³** *n.* mother.
80/3	每		**mei³** see Appendix A.

RADICAL 81

81/0   比   (1)   **pi³** *v.t.* compare.

pi⁴ *v.t.* unite, associate with, assemble, approach, aid; *prep.* by the time of, on behalf of.

RADICAL 83

83/0   氏   (3)   **shih⁴** *n.* surname, family.

83/1   民   (15)   **min²** *n.* people.

RADICAL 85

85/2   求   (6)   **ch'iu²** *v.t.* seek; *n.* demand.

85/3   池   (1)   **ch'ih²** *n.* pool.

85/3   汜   (1)   **ssu⁴** *n.* name of river.

85/5   沮   (2)   **chü³** *v.t.* stop, hinder, prevent.

85/5   況   (2)   **k'uang⁴** *interrog. adv.* how much the more? (note 265).
109y, 127y.

85/5   治   (1)   **chih⁴** *v.i.* be well-governed, be in good order; *v.t.* regulate, arrange, administer, deal with.

85/5   河   (4)   **ho²** *n.* river (especially used with reference to Yellow River); used in 河內 Honei and 河東 Hotung, the names of regions in the state of Wei (Liang).

85/5   泉   (1)   **ch'üan²** *n.* spring, source.

85/5   泣   (1)   **ch'i⁴** *v.i.* weep.

85/6   洿   (1)   **wu¹** *n.* stagnant water, filth, pool.

85/7   涌   (1)   **yung³** *v.i.* bubble up, gush forth.

85/13   激   (1)   **chi¹** *v.t.* dam; *adj.* clear, bright, sharp.

85/14   濟   (2)   **chi⁴** *v.t.* cross a river, carry over a river, help; *v.i.* succeed.

RADICAL 86

86/7   焉   (21)   **yen²** *prep.* + *pron.* (used for 於之 yü² chih¹) in it, on it, from it, than it, etc. (note 19).

yen¹ *interrog. adv.* how?, where?, for what?, in what respect?, whence? (notes 131, 339).
4x, 5b, 7m, 20u, 22k, 30w, 37b, 420, 48u, 54i, 64q, 71s, 100t, 112e, 121t, 129s, 130u, 136v, 138m, 1400, 141p.

86/8   無(无)   (35)   **wu²** *v.t.* not have, lack, there are not (*g.s.* B, notes 32, 52, 221; used in 無乃 wu² nai³, is it not the case that?, surely (note 254); *adv.* used for 毋 wu², do not (note 57).
8p, 12b, 14q, 14x, 16a, 17a, 20l, 21x, 22i, 22q, 26a, 29a, 290, 30l, 32a, 36z, 48f, 50p, 75f, 81k, 86q, 97c, 105q, 106p, 108z, 111e, 113c, 1130, 116z, 120i, 126e, 133m, 135p, 139t.

VOCABULARY

86/8	然	(10)	**jan²** *v.* (used for 如之 ju² chih¹) be like this, do like this; *proclause* this being the case; exactly, quite so, yes; used in 然後 jan² hou⁴, only then; *adv. suffix* -ly (notes 31, 37, 59, 166).
			8j, 9z, 18m, 26i, 28d, 56h, 58f, 60d, 93g, 136n.
86/8	焦	(1)	**chiao¹** *v.i.* burn, scorch; *n.* place in the ancient Chinese state of Chin.
86/9	煖	(1)	**nuan³** *adj.* warm; *v.t.* warm.
86/9	煩	(1)	**fan²** *v.t.* trouble.
86/13	燭	(1)	**chu²** *v.t.* illumine, reflect.

RADICAL 87

87/4	爭	(4)	**cheng¹** *v.t.* strive for, struggle for, contend over.
87/8	為	(44)	**wei²** *v.t.* make, do, play the part of, become, make out to be, regard as; *v.i.* be regarded as, seem; used in 以 . . . 為 i³ wei², q.v. (notes 21, 125, 207, 213, 219, 246).
			wei⁴ *prep.* on behalf of, because of (note 112).

RADICAL 88

| 88/0 | 父 | (9) | **fu⁴** *n.* father. |

RADICAL 89

| 89/10 | 爾 | (3) | **erh³** *personal pron.* you (note 229); used for 而已 erh² i³, and that's all (note 151). |
| | | | 51r, 90g, 119m. |

RADICAL 91

| 91/4 | 版 | (1) | **pan³** *n.* defences. |

RADICAL 93

93/0	牛	(7)	**niu²** *n.* ox.
93/4	物	(1)	**wu⁴** *n.* thing, object, creature.
93/4	牧	(1)	**mu⁴** *v.t.* herd, tend; *n.* pastor, pasturage.
93/7	牽	(1)	**ch'ien¹** *v.t.* pull, drag, lead.

RADICAL 94

94/4	狄	(5)	**ti²** *n.* barbarians of the north.
94/5	狗	(2)	**kou³** *n.* dog.
94/5	狐	(1)	**hu²** *n.* fox.
94/9	猶	(2)	**yu²** *copula* like (app. A); *conj., adv.* still, yet, nevertheless (note 303). 127u, 135i.

94/13	獨	(2)	**tu²** *adv.* alone, only; *adj.* solitary.
94/14	獲	(1)	**huo⁴** *v.t.* seize, capture, obtain, find.
94/15	獸	(1)	**shou⁴** *n.* animal.
94/16	獻	(2)	**hsien⁴** *v.t.* offer up, present.

RADICAL 95

95/6	率	(1)	**shuai⁴** *v.t.* follow, conform to, cause to follow, lead.

RADICAL 96

96/0	王	(39)	**wang²** *n.* king; *adj.* royal, kingly. **wang⁴** *v.i.* be a king, reign.
96/9	瑕	(1)	**hsia²** *n.* flaw, fault; place in the ancient Chinese state of Chin.

RADICAL 99

99/4	甚	(4)	**shen⁴** *adj.* very, extreme, important; *n.* the extreme; *adv.* extremely.

RADICAL 100

100/0	生	(15)	**sheng¹** *v.t.* beget, bear, produce; *v.i.* be born, live; *n.* the living.

RADICAL 101

101/0	用	(11)	**yung⁴** *v.t.* use.

RADICAL 102

102/0	田	(3)	**t'ien²** *n.* field, cultivated land; *v.i.* go hunting.
102/0	甲	(2)	**chia³** *n.* one of the 'ten stems' (cf. 1/3 丑 ch'ou³); armour.
102/0	申	(3)	**shen¹** *n.* one of the 'twelve branches' (cf. 1/3 丑 ch'ou³); *v.t.* extend, stretch, repeat.
102/0	由	(2)	**yu²** *prep.* from (note 115); *v.t.* act in accordance with, follow, go by; *n.* source, cause; used for 猶 yu², q.v. 24d, 36l.
102/5	畝	(2)	**mou³** *n.* a measure of area.
102/5	畜	(1)	**ch'u⁴** *n.* domestic animals. **hsü⁴** *v.t.* rear; *n.* rearing, breeding.
102/6	異	(2)	**i⁴** *v.i.* be different; *adj.* different, strange; *v.t.* consider strange, be surprised at.
102/6	畢		**pi⁴** see Appendix A.
102/8	當	(3)	**tang¹** *v.t.* match, oppose, take on, undertake, act as, suit; *prep.* corresponding to, at, during (app. A).
102/14	疆	(2)	**chiang¹** *n.* boundary, frontier.

RADICAL 104

104/5 疾 (5) **chi²** *v.i.* be ill; *n.* illness, defect; *v.t.* detest; *adv.* quickly, anxiously, violently.

104/5 病 (2) **ping⁴** *n.* illness; *v.i.* be ill, be distressed.

RADICAL 105

105/7 發 (1) **fa¹** *v.t.* shoot, issue, promulgate, distribute.

RADICAL 106

106/0 白 (1) **pai²** *adj.* white; *n.* whiteness.

106/1 百 (13) **pai³** *n., adj.* hundred; used in 百姓 pai³ hsing⁴, 'the hundred surnames', the people.

106/4 皆 (3) **chieh¹** *adv.* all (notes 90, 237, 250).
27n, 97k, 105c.

RADICAL 108

108/4 盈 (1) **ying²** *v.t.* fill.

108/5 益 (4) **i⁴** *v.t.* increase, augment; *n.* profit, advantage; *adv.* increasingly, more (note 188).
69r, 93m, 122o, 137u.

108/5 盍 (4) **ho²** *interrog. adv.* used for 何不 ho² pu⁴, why not? (note 257).
106m, 115p, 121b, 129b.

108/6 盜 (11) **tao⁴** *n.* robber, robbery; *v.t.* steal.

108/6 盛 (3) **sheng⁴** *adj.* abundant, full, complete, successful; *n.* fulness, success.

108/8 盟 (1) **meng²** *n.* treaty, covenant; *v.i.* make a treaty, covenant.

108/9 盡 (1) **chin⁴** *v.t.* fully use, exhaust, entirely devote; *adv.* entirely, fully, utterly (app. A).

108/10 盤 (5) **p'an²** *n.* dish.

RADICAL 109

109/0 目 (3) **mu⁴** *n.* eye.

109/3 直 (1) **chih²** *adj.* straight, upright; *v.t.* straighten, put right; *adv.* only, merely.

109/4 相 (1) **hsiang¹** *v.t.* assist, minister to; *n.* minister; *adv.* in cooperation, together; *pronominal adv.* each other (note 305).
128s.

109/8 睦 (1) **mu⁴** *adj.* harmonious, friendly; *n.* concord.

109/9 睹 (1) **tu³** *v.t.* see.

109/10 瞋 (1) **ch'en¹** *v.* glare (usually with 目 mu⁴ as object).

RADICAL 111

111/2   矣   (31)   **i³** *final particle* indicating action of verb is complete or happens once and for all (*g.s.* A.2, notes 13, 25, 210, 295).
2m, 3t, 5g, 6r, 7o, 15t, 16l, 17c, 17y, 23d, 27k, 35c, 55v, 56f, 57t, 58d, 59q, 60w, 81s, 99c, 107q, 112a, 115d, 122l, 124c, 126b, 128x, 134n, 135o, 137o, 140d.

111/3   知   (18)   **chih¹** *v.t.* know, understand.

RADICAL 113

113/3   祀   (2)   **ssu⁴** *n.* sacrifice; *v.t.* sacrifice to.

113/5   祖   (2)   **tsu³** *n.* ancestor.

113/6   祭   (2)   **chi⁴** *n.* sacrifice; *v.t.* sacrifice to.

113/8   祿   (2)   **lu⁴** *n.* salary, emolument, recompense.

113/11   禦   (1)   **yü⁴** *v.t.* withstand, hinder, prevent.

113/13   禮   (2)   **li³** *n.* ceremony, rite, ritual, propriety, courtesy.

RADICAL 114

114/8   禽   (1)   **ch'in²** *n.* bird; *v.t.* capture, catch.

RADICAL 115

115/5   秦   (8)   **ch'in²** *n.* name of an ancient Chinese state.

115/6   移   (2)   **i²** *v.t.* move, transfer, alter.

115/9   稱   (2)   **ch'eng¹** *v.t.* style, address as, call, praise, recommend, state, declare, mention.

115/10   穀   (2)   **ku³** *n.* grain; *adj.* good, worthy.

RADICAL 116

116/0   穴   (1)   **hsüeh⁴** *n.* hole, cave.

116/17   竊   (3)   **ch'ieh⁴** *v.t.* steal: *adv.* stealthily, secretly, privately, humbly, deferentially (note 215).
82p, 100m, 127q.

RADICAL 117

117/0   立   **li⁴** *v.i.* stand; *v.t.* establish, set up.

117/6   章   (1)   **chang¹** *n.* ornament, pattern, stanza, distinctive mark; *v.t.* ornament, display, manifest, illustrate.

RADICAL 118

118/4   笑   (2)   **hsiao⁴** *v.t.* laugh, laugh at.

RADICAL 119

119/6   粟   (3)   **su⁴** *n.* grain.

RADICAL 120

120/3   紂   (4)   **chou⁴** *n.* last ruler of Shang Dynasty, who came to be regarded as a personification of tyrannical rule.

120/4   索   (1)   **so³** *v.t.* demand.

120/5   終   (2)   **chung¹** *v.t.* end, last to the end; *prep.* throughout; *adj.* whole.

120/6   絕   (3)   **chüeh²** *v.t.* break off, cut off, break off relations with; *adv.* abruptly, decisively.

120/8   維   (1)   **wei²** *v.t.* tie, bind together; *n.* guiding rope of net, guiding principle.

120/9   綿   (1)   **mien²** *adj.* long and thin.

120/10   縋   (1)   **chui⁴** *v.t.* let down by rope.

120/11   縱   **tsung⁴** see Appendix A.

120/11   繆   (1)   **miu⁴** (used for 謬 miu⁴) *n.* error, falsehood; *adj.* deceitful.

120/12   織   (5)   **chih¹** *v.t.* weave.

RADICAL 122

122/5   罟   (1)   **ku³** *n.* net.

122/8   置   (1)   **chih⁴** *v.t.* establish, place, set aside.

122/8   罪   (10)   **tsui⁴** *n.* crime, guilt, offence, blame.

122/10   罷   (1)   **p'i²** *v.t.* wear out, exhaust.
             pa⁴ *v.i.* cease; *v.t.* put a stop to.

RADICAL 123

123/0   羊   (5)   **yang²** *n.* sheep.

123/3   美   (4)   **mei³** *n.* beauty, excellence; *adj.* beautiful, fine, excellent.

123/5   羞   (1)   **hsiu¹** *n.* shame; *v.t.* feel ashamed, be ashamed of.

123/7   羣   **ch'ün²** see Appendix A.

123/7   義   (23)   **i⁴** *n.* duty, righteousness, justice.

RADICAL 124

124/8   翟   (6)   **ti²** *n.* personal name of the philosopher Mo Ti.

124/11   翼   (1)   **i⁴** *n.* wing; capital of the ancient Chinese state called Chin; *v.t.* protect, shelter.

RADICAL 125

125/0   老   (2)   **lao³** *n.,* *adj.* old, elderly; *v.i.* be old; *v.t.* treat as the old should be treated, venerate.

125/5 者 (52) **che³** *particle* used to mark substantival clauses (*g.s.* A.4, notes 16, 26, 32, 54, 59, 92, 107, 112, 242; used in 昔者 hsi² che³ and 或者 huo⁴ che³, qq.v.

RADICAL 126

126/0 而 (92) **erh²** *conj.* and, but (*g.s.* A.5, notes 2, 12, 248, app. A); used in 而巳 (矣) erh² i³ (i³), and that's all (note 11); used in 而後 erh² hou⁴, afterwards, consequently, only then (note 40).

RADICAL 127

127/4 耕 (11) **keng¹** *v.t.* plough.

RADICAL 128

128/0 耳 (6) **erh³** *n.* ear; *final particle* used for 而巳 erh² i³, and that's all (note 29). 7n, 11q, 54f, 54h, 64n, 64p.

128/7 聖 (2) **sheng⁴** *n., adj.* sage.

128/8 聚 (1) **chü⁴** *v.t.* assemble, collect.

128/8 聞 (12) **wen²** *v.t.* hear; *n.* fame.

128/11 聲 (2) **sheng¹** *n.* sound, noise, voice, cry.

128/16 聽 (3) **t'ing¹** *v.t.* listen, listen to, heed, obey.

RADICAL 129

129/7 肆 (1) **ssu⁴** *v.t.* spread out, display, enlarge; *n.* market, shop.

RADICAL 130

130/0 肉 (3) **jou⁴** *n.* meat, flesh.

130/3 肝 (2) **kan¹** *n.* liver.

130/5 胡 (1) **hu²** *interrog. adv.* why? (app. A); 胡齕 Hu Ho is the name of a Ch'i courtier.

130/6 脅 (1) **hsieh²** *n.* ribs.

130/6 能 (26) **neng²** *aux. v.* be able to; *n.* ability (*g.s.* E, notes 77, 327). 23l, 42a, 42p, 44t, 47e, 47s, 56t, 57j, 58s, 59g, 80j, 80s, 80z, 81f, 82l, 83p, 83y, 97v, 109n, 116v, 117c, 118v, 119a, 131f, 135q, 135y.

130/7 脩 (1) **hsiu¹** *n.* dried meat; *v.t.* arrange, cultivate; *adj.* long, tall.

130/7 脣 (2) **ch'un²** *n.* lips.

130/12 膳 (1) **shan⁴** *n.* food.

130/13 膾 (1) **kuei⁴** *v.t.* mince.

RADICAL 131

131/0   臣   **ch'en²** *n.* minister, subject; *quasi-pron.* your servant, I (note 72); *v.t.* treat as minister, make into a minister.
22l, 24j, 27t, 49f, 49q, 72c, 100z, 101a, 135e.

131/8   臧   (3)   **tsang¹** *adj.* good.

131/11 臨   (1)   **lin²** *v.t.* approach, look down on, condescend to, oversee.

RADICAL 132

132/0   自   (2)   **tzu⁴** *prep.* from (note 280); *pronominal adv.* himself (notes 158, 302). 53n, 116p.

132/6   皋落   **kao¹-lo⁴** *n.* name of a barbarian tribe.

RADICAL 133

133/0   至   (5)   **chih⁴** *v.t.* come to, reach, arrive at; *n.* extreme, highest point, utmost, perfection; *adv.* extremely; *prep.* up to, as far as.

RADICAL 134

134/7   與   (16)   **yü³** *v.t.* give; associate with, take part in (note 150); *prep.* together with (note 306); *conj.* and (notes 51, 200).
yü¹ *interrog. particle* used for 也乎 yeh³ hu¹ (note 87).
13w, 26n, 39l, 50t, 51l, 65k, 66z, 77c, 102p, 108a, 117j, 117o, 121n 128v, 131j, 142e.

134/10 舉   **chü³** see Appendix A.

RADICAL 135

135/0   舌   (1)   **she²** *n.* tongue.

135/2   舍   (2)   **she⁴** *v.i.* stop the night, rest, halt, lodge; *n.* lodging place.
she³ *v.t.* put aside, let go, leave alone.

RADICAL 136

136/6   舜   (2)   **shun⁴** *n.* name of a legendary emperor of antiquity.

RADICAL 138

138/1   良   (1)   **liang²** *adj.* good.

RADICAL 140

140/5   苛   (1)   **ho¹** *v.t.* harass, molest, tyrannize.

140/5   若   (20)   **jo⁴** *v.t.* be like, do like (notes 78, 176); *prep.* like (note 310); as for; *conj.* if (note 208).

23p, 25z, 28z, 30i, 61b, 69f, 80w, 84c, 95x, 106j, 112t, 114t, 115h, 121u, 122e, 130i, 134o, 137p, 139a, 141k.

140/5	苟	(3)	**kou³** *conj.* if (note 23); *adv.* carelessly.

5h, 109f, 111m.

140/5	苦	(1)	**k'u³** *adj.* bitter, grievous; *v.t.* suffer, be pained by.
140/6	荆	(1)	**ching¹** *n.* old name for the ancient state called Ch'u.
140/7	莫	(3)	**mo⁴** *pron.* nobody, nothing (notes 76, 152, 156); used in 莫不 mo⁴ pu⁴, everybody.

23j, 51v, 52p.

140/9	萬	(4)	**wan⁴** *n., adj.* ten thousand (note 205).
140/10	蒙	(1)	**meng²** *v.t.* cover, deceive.
140/10	蓋	(1)	**kai⁴** *n.* cover; *v.t.* cover, conceal; *interrog. adv.* used for 何不 ho² pu⁴, why not?, surely (note 257).
140/13	薪	(1)	**hsin¹** *n.* firewood, faggots.
140/13	薄	(1)	**po²** *adj.* light, small, weak; *n.* weakness; *v.t.* press on, fall on, approach.
140/14	藉	(4)	**chieh⁴** *v.t.* avail oneself of, depend on; *conj.* supposing that (note 171).

56z, 58x, 64z, 66l, 72c.

RADICAL 141

141/2	虎	(1)	**hu³** *n.* tiger.
141/5	處	(1)	**ch'u³** *v.t.* dwell, inhabit, remain at home.
			ch'u⁴ *n.* place.

RADICAL 143

143/6	衆	(15)	**chung⁴** *n.* multitude, masses, many; *adj.* numerous, all, many.

RADICAL 144

144/0	行	(11)	**hsing²** *v.t.* do, practice, execute, carry out; *v.i.* function, be active, circulate, go, travel; used in 行李 hsing² li³, traveller, envoy.
			hsing⁴ *n.* conduct.
			hang² *n.* row, rank, column, file.
144/5	術	(1)	**shu⁴** *n.* art, device, skill, trade.
144/9	衛	(1)	**wei⁴** *n.* name of an ancient Chinese state.

RADICAL 145

145/0	衣	(7)	**i¹** *n.* clothes.
			i⁴ *v.t.* wear, clothe.
145/4	衾	(1)	**ch'in¹** *n.* coverlet.
145/5	被	(1)	**pei⁴** *v.t.* receive, suffer.
			p'i⁴ *v.t.* wear (armour).
145/9	褊	(1)	**pien³** *adj.* narrow.

RADICAL 146

146/0	西	(2)	**hsi¹** *n., adj.* west, western.
146/3	要	(1)	**yao¹** *v.t.* seek, intercept; *n.* agreement, compact.
			yao⁴ *adj.* important, principal.

RADICAL 147

147/0	見	(24)	**chien⁴** *v.t.* see, go to see, have an interview with; *aux. v.* putting accompanying verb into passive (app. A).
147/5	視	(1)	**shih⁴** *v.t.* see, regard, behave towards, attend to.
147/9	親	(11)	**ch'in¹** *n.* parent, relative, kinship, affection; *v.t.* be affectionate towards, come close to; *adj.* intimate; *adv.* in person, personally.
147/18	觀	(1)	**kuan¹** *v.t.* inspect, observe.

RADICAL 148

148/9	觳觫	(2)	**hu² su⁴** *n.* frightened appearance, trembling.

RADICAL 149

149/0	言	(18)	**yen²** *n.* word, saying; *v.t.* say, speak, tell, mention.
149/2	計	(1)	**chi⁴** *v.t.* calculate, reckon.
149/4	許	(2)	**hsü³** *v.t.* promise, agree, grant, concede.
149/4	設	(3)	**she⁴** *v.t.* place, arrange, set up; *conj.* supposing that (note 180). 65a, 66m, 140m.
149/5	詔	(4)	**chao⁴** *v.t.* instruct.
149/7	說	(9)	**shuo¹** *v.t.* speak, tell, explain, talk about; *n.* saying, explanation.
			yüeh⁴ (used for 悅 yüeh⁴) *v.i.* be pleased.
149/7	語	(1)	**yü³** *n.* words, speech.
			yü⁴ *v.t.* tell, converse, talk about.
149/7	誣	(1)	**wu¹** *v.t.* deceive, impose on, slander; *n.* deceit, sham.
149/7	誠	(2)	**ch'eng²** *adj.* sincere; *adv.* truly, really.
149/7	誦	(1)	**sung⁴** *v.t.* sing, recite.
149/8	誰	(2)	**shui²** *interrog. pron.* who?, which? (note 298). 126z, 129h.
149/8	請	(8)	**ch'ing³** *v.t.* ask for, request, beg to, invite, intercede for.
149/9	謁	(4)	**yeh⁴** *v.t.* visit a superior, announce, introduce.
149/9	諸	(10)	**chu¹** *adj.* or *collective prefix* all (notes 174, 239, 247); used for 之於 chih¹ yü² (note 167); used for 之乎 chih¹ hu¹ (note 88). 27a, 56p, 58o, 59y, 78e, 97x, 102n, 117t, 118r, 122z.
149/9	謂	(20)	**wei⁴** *v.t.* tell, say that, call, mean.
149/9	諾	(1)	**no⁴** *v.i.* say 'yes', assent, agree.

| 149/11 | 謹 | (1) | **chin³** *adj.* attentive; *v.t.* pay attention to. |
| 149/12 | 識 | (3) | **shih⁴** *v.t.* know. |

RADICAL 151

| 151/3 | 豈 | (5) | **ch'i³** *interrog. adv.* how?, surely not (notes 149, 187). |

50x, 69p, 106z, 109m, 114f.

RADICAL 152

| 152/4 | 豚 | (1) | **t'un²** *n.* young pig. |

RADICAL 154

154/0	貝	(1)	**pei⁴** *n.* cowry shell.
154/2	負	(1)	**fu⁴** *v.t.* carry on the back, turn the back on.
154/3	貢	(1)	**kung⁴** *n.* tribute; *v.t.* pay tribute, present as tribute.
154/3	財	(3)	**ts'ai²** *n.* wealth, resources.
154/4	貪	(2)	**t'an¹** *v.t.* covet, be greedy for; *adj.* covetous, greedy.
154/4	貧	(1)	**p'in²** *adj.* poor; *n.* poverty.
154/5	貴	(3)	**kuei⁴** *n.* honour, high rank; *adj.* noble, honourable; *v.t.* show honour to, esteem.
154/5	貳	(1)	**erh⁴** *v.i.* be divided in allegiance, play false, deviate, be disaffected, transfer allegiance.
154/8	賞	(2)	**shang³** *v.t.* reward.
154/8	賤	(1)	**chien⁴** *n.* low rank; *adj.* base, mean, humble; *v.t.* despise.
154/8	賜	(1)	**tz'u⁴** *v.t.* bestow.
154/8	賢	(3)	**hsien²** *adj.* worthy, talented and virtuous; *n.* man of ability and virtue.
154/9	賴	(1)	**lai⁴** *v.t.* lean on, trust; *n.* reliance, gain, advantage.

RADICAL 156

156/0	走	(4)	**tsou³** *v.i.* go, run, flee.
156/3	起	(2)	**ch'i³** *v.i.* rise, start.
156/5	越	(2)	**yüeh⁴** *v.t.* go beyond; *n.* name of an ancient Chinese state.
156/10	趨	(2)	**ch'ü¹** *v.i.* hasten, rush.

RADICAL 157

| 157/0 | 足 | (8) | **tsu²** *n.* foot; *aux. v.* be capable of, be adequate for, be fit to, be sufficient for (*g.s.* E, notes 89, 150). |

27h, 51k, 74o, 74u, 85p, 85u, 95k, 98w.

| 157/5 | 距 | (1) | **chü⁴** *v.t.* resist. |

157/5	跖	(11)	**chih**[1] *n.* sole of foot.
157/6	路	(2)	**lu**[4] *n.* road.
157/9	踰	(4)	**yü**[2] *v.t.* pass over, transgress, go beyond, exceed.

RADICAL 158

158/0	身	(5)	**shen**[1] *n.* body, person.

RADICAL 159

159/0	車	(1)	**ch'e**[1] *n.* carriage, chariot.
159/2	軍	(9)	**chün**[1] *n.* army; *v.i.* encamp (note 321).
159/5	軻	(1)	**k'o**[1] *n.* personal name of Mencius.
159/7	輕	(1)	**ch'ing**[1] *adj.* light (opposite of heavy), easy; *v.t.* make light of, demean.
159/9	輸	(5)	**shu**[1] *v.t.* transport, convey, contribute, squander, exhaust.
159/9	輯	(1)	**chi**[4] *v.t.* assemble; *n.* harmony; *adj.* harmonious.
159/10	輿	(1)	**yü**[2] *n.* carriage, chariot.

RADICAL 160

160/12	辭	(4)	**tz'u**[2] *n.* words, speech; *v.t.* utter; make excuses, decline, refuse.
160/14	辯	(3)	**pien**[4] *v.t.* dispute, debate, discuss, discriminate; *n.* argument, debate.

RADICAL 161

161/3	辱	(1)	**ju**[4] *v.t.* disgrace, put to shame; *v.i.* condescend.
161/6	農	(2)	**nung**[2] *n.* farming, farmer.

RADICAL 162

162/6	逆	(2)	**ni**[4] *v.t.* meet, go to meet, go against, offend against, disobey, be out of harmony with.
162/6	迷	(1)	**mi**[2] *v.t.* deceive, delude; *v.i.* go astray.
162/6	退	(1)	**t'ui**[4] *v.i.* retire, withdraw, stay in retirement.
162/7	造	(7)	**tsao**[4] *v.t.* make. **ts'ao**[4] *v.t.* go to.
162/7	通	(4)	**t'ung**[1] *v.t.* pass through, penetrate, enter relations with, communicate with; *adj.* all-pervasive, universal, general.
162/8	進	(7)	**chin**[4] *v.i.* go forward, advance; *v.t.* cause to advance, introduce, promote.
162/9	過	(4)	**kuo**[4] *v.t.* go past, go beyond, surpass, transgress; *n.* fault, error.

162/9	道	(6)	**tao⁴** *n.* road, way, method, principles, teaching; *v.t.* explain, talk about, **tao³** *v.t.* lead, govern.
162/9	遇	(2)	**yü⁴** *v.t.* meet, be on good terms with.
162/9	遂	(1)	**sui⁴** *v.t.* advance, continue, accompany, follow; *conj.* thereupon. accordingly, then, thereafter (note 315). 131n
162/9	違	(1)	**wei²** *v.t.* go against, contravene, oppose, deviate from, avoid.
162/10	遠	(3)	**yüan³** *adj.* distant, far, remote; *v.i.* be distant; *v.t.* regard as distant. **yüan⁴** *v.t.* keep at a distance, make remote.
162/12	遺	(1)	**i²** *v.t.* bequeath, transmit, send, neglect, abandon.
162/13	避	(1)	**pi⁴** *v.t.* avoid, escape from.
162/15	邊	(2)	**pien¹** *n.* border, frontier.

RADICAL 163

163/0	邑	(2)	**i⁴** *n.* town, city.
163/4	邪	(1)	**hsieh²** *adj.* crooked, corrupt, depraved. **yeh²** *interrog. particle* used for 也乎 yeh³ hu¹ (note 228). 90b.
163/7	郢	(1)	**ying³** *n.* capital of state of Ch'u.
163/8	郭	(1)	**kuo¹** *n.* outer wall of a city.
163/11	鄙	(4)	**pi³** *n.* border, border area, dependency; *adj.* rustic, poor, mean.
163/12	鄭	(10)	**cheng⁴** *n.* name of an ancient Chinese state.
163/12	鄰	(6)	**lin²** *n.* neighbour; *adj.* neighbouring.

RADICAL 164

164/11	醫	(1)	**i¹** *n.* physician.
164/18	釁	(2)	**hsin⁴** *v.t.* smear with blood in sacrifice; *n.* crevice, opening.

RADICAL 165

165/1	采	(1)	**ts'ai³** *v.t.* gather, pluck; *adj.* variegated.
165/13	釋	(2)	**shih⁴** *v.t.* unloose, let go, give up, unravel, explain.

RADICAL 166

166/0	里	(2)	**li³** *n.* village, neighbourhood, measure of distance (equal to about a third of a mile).
166/2	重	(1)	**chung⁴** *adj.* heavy, important. **ch'ung²** *adj.* double; *v.t.* double, repeat.
166/4	野	(1)	**yeh³** *n.* open country, uncultivated land, wilderness.

RADICAL 167

167/0	金	(1)	**chin**[1] *n.* metal, metal coin.
167/4	鈞	(1)	**chün**[1] *v.t.* balance, be equal to, make equal; *n.* weight of thirty catties.
167/7	銳	(1)	**jui**[4] *adj.* sharp, keen, valiant, quick; *n.* sharp weapon.
167/9	鐘	(2)	**chung**[1] *n.* kind of wine vessel; measure of grain; bell.
167/12	鐘	(1)	**chung**[1] *n.* bell.

RADICAL 168

168/0	長	(4)	**ch'ang**[2] *adj.* long, tall.
			chang[3] *n.* elder, senior; *v.t.* be senior to, be superior to, oversee, preside over; *v.i.* grow up.

RADICAL 169

169/10	闕	(2)	**ch'üeh**[4] *n.* look-out tower, gate, opening, shortcoming, defect; *v.t.* reduce, diminish, omit.

RADICAL 170

170/8	陶	(1)	**t'ao**[2] *n.* pottery, potter; *v.i.* be a potter, practise pottery.
170/8	陪	(1)	**p'ei**[2] *v.t.* double, augment.
170/8	陵	(1)	**ling**[2] *n.* mound, hill; *v.t.* ascend, transgress, encroach upon, molest, oppress.
170/8	陳	(1)	**ch'en**[2] *v.t.* set forth, arrange, display, marshal; *n.* name of an ancient Chinese state.
170/9	陽	(1)	**yang**[2] *n.* male principle in nature (as contrasted with 陰 yin[1], the female principle), south slope of hill, north bank of river.
170/14	隱	(4)	**yin**[3] *v.t.* conceal; suffer, be grieved at; lean on; *v.i.* go into retirement; *adj.* concealed, secret, withdrawn.

RADICAL 172

172/9	雖	(5)	**sui**[2] *conj.* although, even if (notes 93, 216). 28l, 63h, 84p, 112f, 121y.
172/10	雞	(1)	**chi**[1] *n.* fowl.
172/10	雙	(1)	**shuang**[1] *n.* pair, peer, match.
172/11	難	(3)	**nan**[2] *n.* difficulty, crisis, calamity; *adj.* difficult.

RADICAL 173

173/4	雲	(1)	**yün**[2] *n.* cloud.

RADICAL 175

175/0 非 (10) **fei¹** *negative copula* is not (*g.s.* B, notes 61, 153, 227, 298); *prep.* contrary to; *v.t.* reject, condemn; *adj.* wrong.
19q, 20f, 31g, 39x, 41x, 52a, 85x, 90a, 91s, 126w.

RADICAL 176

176/0 面 (2) **mien⁴** *n.* face; *v.t.* face, look towards.

RADICAL 180

180/0 音 (1) **yin¹** *n.* sound, note.

RADICAL 181

181/3 順 (2) **shun⁴** *v.t.* follow, obey, accord with, submit to; *n.* harmony.

181/9 顏 (1) **yen²** *n.* countenance.

181/10 願 (3) **yüan⁴** *n., aux. v.* wish, desire.
72d, 94b, 103r.

181/10 類 (1) **lei⁴** *n.* class, category; *adj.* belonging to the same class, similar, fitting, proper; *v.t.* classify.

181/12 顧 (1) **ku⁴** *v.t.* look at, turn towards, have regard for.

181/14 顯 (1) **hsien³** *adj.* manifest, conspicuous; *v.t.* display; *v.i.* be illustrious.

RADICAL 182

182/0 風 (2) **feng¹** *n.* wind, manners, customs; *v.i.* face the wind; be on heat.

182/11 飄 (1) **p'iao¹** *n.* whirlwind.

RADICAL 184

184/0 食 (14) **shih²** *v.t.* eat; *n.* food; eclipse.
ssu⁴ *v.t.* feed.

184/5 飽 (1) **pao³** *v.i.* eat one's fill, be satisfied; *v.t.* provide sufficient to eat for, satiate.

184/5 飾 (1) **shih⁴** *v.t.* adorn, decorate, gloss over; *n.* ornament.

184/6 養 (3) **yang³** *v.t.* nourish, support.

184/7 餘 (2) **yü²** *n.* remnant, surplus; used after numerals to mean 'a few extra', like 'odd' in 'seventy-odd'.

184/7 餓 (1) **o⁴** *v.i.* be famished, starve; *adj.* starving.

184/7 餔 (2) **pu³** *v.t.* eat.
pu¹ *n.* evening meal.

184/12 饑 (4) **chi¹** *v.i.* be hungry; *adj.* hungry; *n.* hunger, famine.

184/14 饜 (1) **yen⁴** *v.i.* be satisfied.

RADICAL 187

187/0	馬	(1)	**ma**[3] *n.* horse.
187/5	駕	(1)	**chia**[4] *v.t.* yoke, harness.
187/11	驅	(1)	**ch'ü**[1] *v.i.* gallop, hasten; *v.t.* drive.
187/13	驚	(1)	**ching**[1] *v.i.* be frightened; *v.t.* frighten.
187/19	驪姬		**li**[2] **chi**[1] *n.* name of a wife of Duke Hsien of Chin.

RADICALS 189–211

189/0	高	(1)	**kao**[1] *adj.* high, lofty.
190/5	髮	(1)	**fa**[3] *n.* hair.
195/0	魚	(2)	**yü**[2] *n.* fish.
195/4	魯	(6)	**lu**[3] *n.* name of an ancient Chinese state.
201/0	黃	(1)	**huang**[2] *n., adj.* yellow.
202/3	黎	(1)	**li**[2] *adj.* numerous; black, black-haired.
205/12	鼈	(2)	**pieh**[1] *n.* turtle.
206/0	鼎	(2)	**ting**[3] *n.* type of sacrificial vessel, cauldron.
207/0	鼓	(6)	**ku**[3] *n.* drum; *v.t.* make a drumming movement with, drum (soldiers) into action.
210/0	齊	(8)	**ch'i**[2] *adj.* uniform, equal, even, regular; *n.* name of an ancient Chinese state.
211/0	齒	(1)	**ch'ih**[3] *n.* teeth; old age, seniority.

LIST OF CHARACTERS HAVING OBSCURE RADICALS

Characters whose radicals may be difficult for the beginner to determine are listed here, arranged according to the total number of strokes with which the characters are written.

2		丹	3/3	尺	44/1	本	75/1
七	1/1	之	4/3	弔	57/1	未	75/1
乃	4/1	予	6/3			正	77/1
九	5/1	云	7/2	**5**		母	80/1
		五	7/2	世	1/4	民	83/1
3		今	9/2	且	1/4	甲	102/0
上	1/2	介	9/2	丘	1/4	申	102/0
下	1/2	内	11/2	主	3/4	由	102/0
也	5/2	公	12/2	乏	4/4		
于	7/1	凶	17/2	乎	4/4	**6**	
亡	8/1	勿	20/2	以	9/3	交	8/4
凡	16/1	四	23/2	冬	15/3	亦	8/4
千	24/1	升	24/2	出	17/3	共	12/4
巳	49/0	午	24/2	北	21/3	再	13/4
才	64/0	反	29/2	半	24/3	危	26/4
		友	29/2	去	28/3	在	32/3
4		及	29/2	失	37/2	多	36/3
不	1/3	夫	37/1	平	51/2	成	62/2
丑	1/3	少	42/1	弗	57/2	曳	73/2
中	2/3			必	61/1	有	74/2

死 78/2
求 85/2
百 106/1

7

兵 12/5
吳 30/4
君 30/4
坐 32/4
壯 33/4
孝 39/4
弟 57/4
我 62/3
更 73/3
李 75/3
每 80/3
矣 111/2
良 138/1

8

事 6/7
來 9/6
兩 11/6
其 12/6

函 17/6
卒 24/6
命 30/5
夜 36/5
妾 38/5
季 39/5
尚 42/5
幸 51/5
或 62/4
東 75/4
果 75/4
步 77/4
武 77/4
直 109/3
舍 135/2
采 165/1

9

冠 14/7
前 18/7
南 24/7
即 26/7
哉 30/6
威 38/6

拜 64/5
既 71/5
泉 85/5
甚 99/4
美 123/3
者 125/5
軍 159/2
重 166/2

10

乘 4/9
倉 9/8
兼 12/8
夏 35/7
奚 37/7
師 50/7
席 50/7
秦 115/5
索 120/4
能 130/6
荊 140/6
豈 151/3

11

執 32/8

堂 32/8
孰 39/8
將 41/8
畫 72/7
望 74/7
梁 75/7
馬 86/7
牽 93/7
率 95/6
異 102/6
畢 102/6
羞 123/5
脩 130/7
脣 130/7

12

勝 19/10
喜 30/9
喪 30/9
善 30/9
堯 32/9
就 43/9
幾 52/9
麁 58/9

斑	67/8	禽	114/8	**15**		**17**
棄	75/8	義	123/7	憂	61/11	戴	62/14
為	87/8	聖	128/7	暴	72/11	舉	134/10
發	105/7			樂	75/11	與	159/10
舜	136/6	**14**		穀	115/10		
貳	154/5	嘗	30/11	縣	120/9	**18–25**
		幕	50/11	魯	195/4	歸	77/14
13		爾	89/10	黎	202/3	疆	102/14
弒	56/10	聚	128/8			聽	128/16
愛	61/9	藏	131/8	**16**		纛	164/18
楚	75/9	與	134/7	嚴	148/9		
歲	77/9	養	184/6	賴	154/9